MAKE YOURSELF UNFORGETTABLE

Also available from Dale Carnegie Training

Leadership Mastery

5 Essential People Skills

Stand and Deliver

MAKE YOURSELF UNFORGETTABLE

How to Become the Person Everyone Remembers and No One Can Resist

DALE CARNEGIE TRAINING

SIMON & SCHUSTER

London · New York · Sydney · Toronto

A CBS COMPANY

First published in Great Britain by Simon & Schuster UK Ltd, 2011
This paperback edition published by Simon & Schuster UK Ltd, 2012
A CBS COMPANY

7 9 10 8

Simon & Schuster UK Ltd
1st Floor
222 Gray's Inn Road
London
WC1X 8HB

www.simonandschuster.co.uk

Simon & Schuster Australia, Sydney
Simon & Schuster India, New Delhi

A CIP catalogue for this book is available
from the British Library.

ISBN: 978-0-85720-679-4

Printed and bound in India by Replika Press Pvt. Ltd.

Contents

Introduction

There's a good chance you're already familiar with the poem shown below. It is, after all, one of the most widely read poems in the English language—and it could legitimately be called "the world's most popular poem."

"If" was published by Rudyard Kipling in 1909. Kipling said it was inspired by the exploits of a British officer in South Africa, but today it transcends any specific time or place. Here at the start of our book on the principles of class and the concept of making yourself unforgettable, there can be no better introduction than Rudyard Kipling's poem. You may want to read it again as you go through the book. In fact, you may want to return to it many times as you proceed through your life as a whole. . . .

If you can keep your head when all about you
Are losing theirs and blaming it on you;
If you can trust yourself when all men doubt you,
But make allowance for their doubting too;
If you can wait and not be tired by waiting,
Or, being lied about, don't deal in lies,
Or, being hated, don't give way to hating,
And yet don't look too good, nor talk too wise:

If you can dream—and not make dreams your master;
If you can think—and not make thoughts your aim;
If you can meet with Triumph and Disaster
And treat those two impostors just the same;
If you can bear to hear the truth you've spoken

Twisted by knaves to make a trap for fools,
Or watch the things you gave your life to broken,
And stoop and build 'em up with wornout tools;

If you can make one heap of all your winnings
And risk it on one turn of pitch-and-toss,
And lose, and start again at your beginnings
And never breathe a word about your loss;
If you can force your heart and nerve and sinew
To serve your turn long after they are gone,
And so hold on when there is nothing in you
Except the Will which says to them: "Hold on!";

If you can talk with crowds and keep your virtue,
Or walk with Kings—nor lose the common touch;
If neither foes nor loving friends can hurt you;
If all men count with you, but none too much;
If you can fill the unforgiving minute
With sixty seconds' worth of distance run,
Yours is the Earth and everything that's in it,
And—which is more—you'll be a Man, my son!

This is not a sugarcoated picture of what the world is like! As Kipling depicts it, life is no day at the beach. You're going to be lied to, cheated, blamed, backstabbed, disappointed, and a positive outcome is not guaranteed. Even if you get through all of this, Kipling doesn't provide assurance that you'll find wealth or health or wisdom. He does say you'll get "the Earth and everything that's in it." But what is that supposed to mean? Does anyone even want "the Earth and everything that's in it"?

However, whatever you may get or not get, Kipling does make a promise about what you'll *be.* You'll be a man. Or, rather, you'll be a *Man.* But once again, as with "the Earth and everything that's in it," we need to ask what Kipling intends that to mean.

The answer to that question will be helpful for our understanding of the meaning of class. If being a Man is the payoff for all the trials and tribulations of earthly existence, it must be about much more than gender. Really, it's about wisdom. If you read the poem carefully, you can see that each stanza describes several tests—to which the *right* answer is always the *hard* answer. Why is the hard answer the right one? Again, there's no promise of any material payoff. There's just the state of being you'll eventually attain. And if we want to be consistent with the universe the poem has created, chances are no one will even acknowledge that you're a Man except you yourself.

Perhaps that's the last test, and it sounds like the toughest.

Ultimately, the real payoff for class comes down to self-respect. People with class *know* they're people with class, even if no one else is paying attention. As someone once said, "Who are you when nobody's looking?" When, from the bottom of your heart, you can answer, "I'm the person I really hope and want to be," then you've achieved the goal that is the subject of this book. And again, it may also be the purpose of your life as a whole.

So, onward. . . .

CHAPTER ONE

The Unforgettable Energy

Class—that unique energy that makes people truly unforgettable—is easier to recognize than it is to define. We know it when we see it—but what is "it"? This book will not only help you answer that question, but also to really be a "class act" in every area of your life. When you do this—and it isn't easy—you will literally make yourself unforgettable.

(By the way, just as class is easy to recognize, the absence of class is also easy to detect in a man or a woman. That's not something you want people to see in you!)

We'll have much more to say about what class is and why it's important in the chapters that follow. You'll have a chance to evolve your own definition of class—and you'll gain practical, powerful tools for making yourself unforgettable to everyone you meet. Whether it's in business or in any other area of life, nothing is more valuable than that. You may not realize the full importance of class right now, but when you reach the last page of this book, you most definitely will.

We'll begin by looking at the often unclear meaning of class, as well as the *very clear* effect it can have in both business and personal interactions. We'll see how class was really the deciding factor at a critical moment in American history, and we'll explore how you can make the lessons of that moment work for you.

In subsequent chapters, we'll explore essential elements that compose class in the truest sense of the word. Lastly, in the book's final chapter, we'll look at how class expresses itself through achievement in the material world—for you and also for those around you. This ability to create success for others is one of the most admirable qualities of class. Like a great athlete, a class person always plays the game at a high level and makes better players of his or her teammates as well.

To begin our exploration of class and what it can do, let's look at a case in point. There has never been a clearer example of class in action than history's first presidential debate. The debate took place on September 26, 1960. The participants were John F. Kennedy, then a senator from Massachusetts, and Vice President Richard M. Nixon.

Over the years, whole books have been written about this event, but it's rarely been discussed from the perspective of class in the way that we'll be using the word. Yet class was a huge factor in the debate. It made the difference in who won and who lost, and in that sense it changed the course of history.

John F. Kennedy and Richard Nixon were both in excellent form at the time of their televised encounter. Each of them had good reason to feel optimistic about the election. Their résumés were very different, but were impressive in their different ways.

Each candidate in 1960 had been nominated on the first ballot at his party's national convention. Kennedy, whose nomination had come first, had won impressive victories over the more experienced Senator Hubert Humphrey in the primaries. Kennedy's wins in West Virginia and Wisconsin had made an important point about his chances for gaining the presidency, since there had been some doubt about whether a Roman Catholic could actually win an election outside a predominantly Catholic state such as Massachusetts.

Kennedy's religion had given rise to uncertainty within his party, but the Democrats more or less forgot those worries after West Virginia and Wisconsin. Then, immediately after his nomination, Kennedy made a bold and politically practical move in his selection of a running mate. His choice of Texas senator Lyndon Johnson may have surprised Kennedy's core supporters in the Northeast, but now the Democrats had a powerful national ticket. Johnson, who was the Senate majority leader, was a supremely experienced politician who knew Washington inside and out. He was definitely a fighter, and usually he was a winner.

Perhaps the only drawback to Johnson's selection as the vice-presidential nominee was that he and Kennedy could hardly stand each other! But Kennedy put aside his emotions to make an effective practical decision. Was that a "classy" move? We'll come back to that question later in this chapter.

Two weeks after Kennedy's convention, Richard Nixon became the Republican nominee. In light of what the future held for him when the Watergate scandal broke, it may be difficult to grasp how popular Nixon was at the time of his nomination. In those years America was preoccupied with the nuclear threat from the Soviet Union. Nixon had won huge acclaim when he forcefully argued with the Russian premier Nikita Khrushchev at a trade-show exhibit. He had also faced down a large anti-American mob during a visit to Venezuela. Nixon seemed to offer security and competence at a frightening time in American history. True, he'd already had a few embarrassing moments. But he'd always come out whole and on top. And it seemed as if he would again. He was definitely the favorite to win the general election.

The actual positions presented by Kennedy and Nixon were similar in some respects and very different in others. Both spoke of America's greatness in more or less conventional terms. But Kennedy challenged people's complacency while somehow still sounding positive. In many of his speeches he referred to a "missile gap"—a supposed advantage the Russians possessed in the number of intercontinental weapons. No such gap existed, but, as with his selection of Lyndon Johnson, Kennedy seemed willing to sacrifice certain things to gain his objectives.

In light of the Republican Party's generally hard line on

defense issues, it may be difficult to imagine Richard Nixon as a dove. But compared to Kennedy, that's how he seemed in the 1960 election. Not long before, President Eisenhower—who had been the supreme Allied commander in the war against Nazi Germany—had warned against the growth of a "military industrial complex" that was threatening to dominate American life. Eisenhower's speech on this topic was worthy of the most ardent dove, and Kennedy may actually have agreed with most of it. But instead, he cast himself as the defender of America's freedom against the Soviet military threat.

As the incumbent vice president, Nixon's campaign speeches always referred to a secure present and a brighter future, but he spoke of this in the context of Republican principles such as free enterprise and decreased government spending. Besides the overall message of pro-Americanism, Kennedy and Nixon shared wariness of the Soviet threat and agreed on other foreign-policy issues, although Kennedy put more emphasis on the need to strengthen the military. The similarity of the two candidates' stated beliefs forced the campaigns to seek out ways to distinguish one from the other.

The election turned into a debate about experience. Both candidates had come to Congress in the same year, 1946, but Nixon tried to strengthen his qualifications by playing up his foreign-policy credentials as vice president. The experience issue seemed to be a weak spot in Kennedy's campaign, and before the first debate Nixon seemed to be gaining strength. This was crucial because at the time the number of Democrats was far larger than the number of Republicans nationwide. The race for the White House was so tight that any small advantage could pay enormous dividends.

But just as Nixon was finding his strength, several media events took place that had a strong bearing on the outcome of the election.

Nixon's focus on his experience in foreign and domestic policy was damaged by his own boss. In the fall of 1960, President Eisenhower was holding a press conference, an activity he had never enjoyed. He was in a hurry to get it over with. Then a correspondent asked what major decisions Vice President Nixon had taken part in making. Eisenhower responded, "If you give me a week, I might think of one." The president was not really trying to slight Nixon. He was trying to make a joke about his own weariness and lack of focus. But the remark was a godsend to Kennedy. It gave him a chance to undercut the whole issue of Nixon's superior experience. Kennedy said, "Yes, Mr. Nixon is experienced—but his experience is in the policies of retreat, defeat, and weakness."

Some other problems started to crop up for Mr. Nixon as well. After the Republican National Convention, he had promised to campaign in all fifty states, but a knee infection sidelined him for two weeks. Then against the advice of his inner circle, he returned to the campaign in less than perfect health. And now the tired candidate had to turn his attention to the first-ever televised presidential debate. Nixon had been a champion scholastic debater and welcomed the opportunity to speak with his opponent on national TV, but as the evening played out, the subtleties of media politics lined up against the vice president.

Kennedy devoted a tremendous amount of time preparing for this event. The recent success of his televised answers about religion proved that the medium had immense potential for his success. In addition, a strong showing against the highly favored Nixon would establish credibility on the issues and further boost public confidence in his leadership ability. The vice president also came prepared, but the outcome of the debate would not be decided by substance.

Nixon also ran into bad luck on other media fronts. Kennedy scored well with blacks when he came to the aid of Martin Luther King Jr. after an arrest in Atlanta. The vice president was caught in a conflict of interest and had to remain silent on the well-publicized event. Kennedy used the press coverage to fortify his compassionate, charismatic image. Late in the race, Eisenhower stepped up his support for Nixon. This action was balked at by the Democrats and possibly made the vice president look incapable of winning the election on his own. The perceived weakness was eventually echoed in the press. Combined with Nixon's poor showing in the first debate, the Eisenhower gaffe, and previous triumphs by Kennedy in the media, small press-related miscalculation such as these took their toll on the Republican nominee.

JFK was able to put Nixon on the defensive with his unexpected grasp of the facts, but Nixon held his own in responding to the Kennedy criticisms. The major story of the debate became the visual appeal of the attractive Kennedy versus the sickly look of the worn-down Nixon. Several factors contributed to Nixon's poor image. His health problems leading up to the debate had resulted in severe weight loss. A freshly painted backdrop on the set had dried in a light shade of gray that blended with the color of his suit. During cutaways, the cameras caught Nixon wiping perspiration from his forehead. He looked cornered and rattled. Meanwhile Kennedy looked great in front of the camera.

It's often been pointed out that people who heard the debate on radio thought that Richard Nixon had won, while the millions who watched on TV considered John Kennedy the clear winner. There's a simple reason for this. Nixon had an excellent presentation, but Kennedy had—or seemed to have—an overwhelming *class* advantage.

What do we mean by class advantage? It doesn't mean that Kennedy was wealthier than Nixon, although that was certainly the case. What it *does* mean is the first important point to understand about class. John Kennedy's class advantage came in that he seemed *cool*, *calm*, and in *control*. Nixon may have had the content, but Kennedy had the class. Actually, nothing said that night was particularly significant in terms of public policy or world affairs.

There were no zingers or sound bites, and the issues that were discussed seem totally irrelevant in today's world. But what have endured are images of a relaxed and confident-looking John F. Kennedy—clearly the class act, despite that Richard Nixon was much more experienced in government and much better known.

How did this happen? Amid all that has been written about the first presidential debate, three points stand out. We'll be returning to these points in various forms throughout the book, so as you listen to them now, give some thought to how they may also be present in your life and your career. You may never run for president, but you will surely be facing some of the same decisions Kennedy and Nixon made some fifty years ago. On the surface, those decisions may have seemed to be about technicalities or procedures, but they were really about something else. They were about class—or the perception of class—and about how to most effectively communicate that impression.

First, the participants in the debate were there for very different reasons. For Kennedy, the debate was a positive choice. As a relative unknown, he had everything to gain and little to lose. For Nixon, however, it was a *constraint.* Worst of all, he imposed the constraint upon himself, against the counsel of those around him. Nixon's advisers urged him not to debate Kennedy, but Nixon felt compelled to do so. He felt he had something to prove, perhaps to himself more than to anyone else. So his actions were based on insecurity rather than strength.

This is an extremely interesting dynamic—one that can affect any decision-maker, regardless of the external circumstances. The more powerful people become, the more constrained they may feel to prove that they actually deserve their power. They need constant reassurance and support, which often manifests itself in a crew of yes-men so they can head off any self-doubt.

Class never expresses itself unwillingly. Class is always a positive, or even a joyful, choice. Even if your actions are objectively class, the positive effect is canceled if the motivation is negative.

And make no mistake: negative motivation always reveals itself, sometimes in unexpected and embarrassing ways.

There is an essential link between class and communication. Class acts are people who can clearly communicate who they are and what their vision is. You don't have to be the smartest person in the room to be the leader. It is widely accepted by many historians that two of the brightest men to hold the presidency in recent history were Jimmy Carter and Richard Nixon. Carter had a degree in electrical engineering, and Nixon had a law degree from Duke. Yet whether or not you agreed with his politics, Ronald Reagan is remembered as a popular and effective president, the man responsible for winning the Cold War, the Great Communicator. When he said, "Tear down that wall," he made himself unforgettable. It wasn't because of any academic degrees he'd earned. It was just because of what he said and how he said it.

Unforgettable people speak in terms of vision. Often, surprisingly enough, it's not about what they've done or will do. It's about what they can *see.* They paint the picture of a world that others can't imagine, and they share their vision with words. They don't use statistics to make their point; they use vivid imagery.

Being a great communicator requires two distinct qualities. The first is optimism. Pessimism has no class. An unforgettable person looks beyond any current situation to imagine a better time. When will that time come into being? How will it happen? Those are mere details!

Second, a great communicator puts that shared vision into simple words that everyone can understand. It doesn't help to use a big vocabulary. It does help to use language that can be clearly understood by a truck driver and a scientist—simple, understandable, and repeatable.

Phrases such as *I can see* or *I imagine* or *I believe* are powerful tools. Your thoughts help paint a picture of that image. For example, it does no good to quote statistics showing that when people enjoy going to work their overall productivity and general happiness improve. No one will listen attentively if you assert the importance of developing a series of systems and processes to steadily increase people's enjoyment of work, so that quality gets better. Those are accurate statements, but who would be inspired by them?

But suppose you said this:

"I imagine a time not too far from now in which every single person who goes to work loves what they do. This is the world I can see. Can you imagine going to work every single day and loving what you do and the people you work with? How do you think that would impact your work or even your personal life? This is the world I imagine and it is possible if we work together to create it. Join me. Choose to lead. Choose to inspire. If you do, I know we will be successful. If you lead those around you, if you inspire the people around you, every one of us will wake up and love going to work. Are you in or are you out?"

The meaning is the same, but the message is very different.

"Ask not what your country can do for you, ask what you can do for your country," said John F. Kennedy in his inaugural address in 1961. Why was this unforgettable? Why was *he* unforgettable? Kennedy did not ask us to follow, nor did he ask us to lead. He *challenged* us to serve. This is the irony of an authentic class act. Truly inspiring and unforgettable people aren't driven to lead people. They are driven to serve them. This subtle twist of logic earns a good leader the loyalty and respect of those who ultimately serve them back. For people to be unforgettable, they need a following. Why should any individuals want to follow another individual unless they feel that person would serve them and their interests?

The more you are able to do that, the more you will earn the trust of everyone around you. Not because you're "the boss," but because you know what people need and you are determined to see that they get it.

An unforgettable person wants to help others become the best versions of themselves. An unforgettable person does not propose to do others' work for them. Again, the unforgettable person paints a picture of how others can do it for themselves.

And by the way, that's exactly the intention of this book! So please go on to chapter 2.

CHAPTER TWO

Class in a Crisis

In all areas of life, things happen that seem to be beyond our control or responsibility. During a windstorm, your neighbor's tree falls onto the roof of your house—or, even worse, your tree falls onto your neighbor's house. One person becomes ill, while another stays healthy. Joe wins the lottery, while Jim loses his ticket. So much of life is random. So much of it is simply the luck of the draw.

Well, that may be true, but from the perspective of class, it's not the way to act! If you truly intend to be a class act, if you truly want to make yourself unforgettable, you must accept 100 percent responsibility. You should certainly accept responsibility for yourself, and you should even be able to accept it for other people when they are not in a position to do so. And ultimately, you should even accept it for things that seem obviously outside your control. You may not have caused the tree to blow down, but maybe you could have seen that it could possibly happen if the wind was strong enough. Needless to say, this is a tall order. It isn't easy. It doesn't happen by itself. But it is the class way to look at things.

But that's not all. You not only have to accept total responsibility. You have to make it look easy. If you feel like acting with class is a struggle, you have to hide that struggle at all costs.

Consider this story. Ted drove a truck for a small, family-owned manufacturing company. His wife was about to have a baby. During the delivery, some complications developed that eventually translated into a $20,000 hospital bill. Although his wife and his child were now healthy, Ted had to deal with a real financial problem. Some fine print in his insurance coverage at work raised a question about whether the hospital bill would be covered, and the answer seemed to be no. That, at least, was what the insurance company was telling Ted.

Since there was no way Ted could come up with $20,000, he went to see Warren, the owner of the company Ted worked for. Warren listened to Ted's problem and said that he would call the insurance company himself. It certainly seemed as if Ted's expenses should be covered, and if they weren't, Warren would definitely find out why.

A few days later, Warren ran into Ted at the start of the workday. "I've got some good news," Warren said. "I talked to the insurance company and they've agreed to cover your hospital expenses. You won't be getting any more bills."

Ted thanked his boss profusely. He really appreciated the way Warren had gone to bat for him. Warren died several years later, and at the funeral Ted told Warren's wife what had happened. That was when Ted learned the truth: Warren had personally paid the hospital bill. He could afford it, of course, so the money wasn't really a worry. The only thing that had worried Warren was the possibility that Ted might find out that he'd paid the bill. Taking financial responsibility for someone who needed help was a class act, but letting anyone know about it would definitely not have been.

People with class don't like to see anyone uncomfortable. It doesn't matter whether the discomfort comes from a serious problem, as in Ted's case, or from something relatively minor. The famous songwriter and composer Cole Porter, for example, was renowned for being a class act in every respect. He loved to entertain his friends at his apartment in the Waldorf-Astoria Hotel in New York. On one such occasion, a guest of Porter's was admiring his collection of fine crystal glassware. Suddenly there was a crash. The guest had dropped an antique bowl worth several thousand dollars. A moment before there had been laughter and singing. Now there was dead silence as Cole Porter rose from the piano and approached the horrified guest. "Oh, did you drop a bowl?" he said as he picked up another piece from his collection. "It's an easy mistake to make. They're so slippery." Then, accidentally on purpose, he dropped the second bowl. "Whoops, now I've done it myself," Porter remarked with a grin. "Like I said, it happens all the time. Don't worry about it. In fact, welcome to the club."

How would you have handled that situation? Would the possible embarrassment or discomfort of your guest have been uppermost in your mind? Or would you have worried about the cost of the broken glass and whether you could replace it? Would you have taken responsibility for setting the situation right, even though it wasn't your fault? In short, would you have responded just like the average person—or would you have been a class act?

Class always finds ways to reveal itself, but the real test of a class act comes when catastrophe strikes. For this reason, people with class train themselves to regard problems as opportunities. It may sound like a cliché, but some individuals live by this precept—and those people are truly unforgettable. The late W. Clement Stone, who created a billion-dollar empire in the insurance business, had a unique way of reacting to bad news. As a matter of personal discipline, he trained himself to exclaim, "Excellent!" no matter how dire the information might seem. Stone was determined to find the positive opportunity hidden in every disaster. If there was no hidden opportunity, he would create one.

As we've said, it isn't easy. But it's not supposed to be easy.

In 1982, eight people died when someone put poison in bottles of Tylenol that were sold in a Chicago drugstore. The CEO of Johnson & Johnson immediately took full responsibility for what had happened, even though the company had nothing to do with the poisoning of their product. More than 31 million bottles of Tylenol were taken off the shelves and destroyed, at a cost of $100 million. Was this a good decision? At the time, the CEO of Johnson & Johnson was James Burke. As he put it, "The test of an executive and of a company is how it reacts to catastrophe." In other words, confronting difficult problems is not just something you're forced to do. It's the reason you are *where* you are, and it's a chance to show *who* you are and *what* you are.

It's a matter of setting a higher standard for yourself, and then living up to it—which is not a bad start toward a definition of what "class act" really means.

APPEARANCE AND REALITY

The clinical psychologist Taibi Kahler, Ph.D., has done some insightful studies on human motivation. Specifically, Kahler has identified a number of specific beliefs that cause people to take action in their lives—sometimes with positive results, but often with self-sabotaging results. When people behave in ways that seem to lack true class, it's not because they intend to do so. On the contrary, their motivation may be quite positive, but also misguided. To understand how this works, studying Taibi Kahler's four motivating drives can be helpful.

Kahler identifies the first motivating drive as the need to be "perfect." That means, as Kahler puts it, "You must be perfect. You must be correct in every way. You must succeed in everything you do. And you must always win."

We can see how this belief affected Richard Nixon in his first presidential debate. He felt compelled to participate, to meet the challenge, and to win—despite the many obvious reasons for doing otherwise. He wanted to be a "class act," which in itself is a positive intention. The problem was, he was acting out of fear. He was afraid of being seen as less than perfect. Unfortunately, that is exactly how he came to be seen.

Other potentially self-sabotaging drives include:

- The wish to seem strong at all times. This is based on a fundamental misunderstanding, that is, that never showing vulnerability equates with strength.
- A feeling of urgency and a need to be "in the lead" at all times. While a significant number of very successful people were identified as outstanding from the beginning, many more were not. The need to be "the youngest millionaire" or "the top performer under the age of thirty" is a trap no one should fall into. Yet many people do.
- The desire to please others at all costs, and to have this validated by acknowledgment and praise. Deserving and receiving recognition can be worthy impulses, but not when you need others to tell you whether you have done well. Similarly, it's good to be accommodating of others' wishes, but not when there's an underlying belief that you're not "good enough" unless other people are pleased with you.

THE CARNEGIE CONNECTION

Although the word *class* does not often appear in his books, the concepts that we're discussing here are fundamental to Dale Carnegie's work and to the impact he's had on millions of people's lives. Let's look right now at some of what Dale Carnegie had to say along these lines. I think you'll see how closely related these ideas are to the ideas we've looked at so far—especially the importance of accepting responsibility, and seeing that responsibility as an opportunity rather than a burden.

As we've said, this isn't rocket science. Class doesn't need to be complicated. In the Nixon-Kennedy debates, we saw how some basic ideas about making a good first impression and appropriate behavior turned out to be hugely important.

How do you feel about the way you dress, for example? Do you regard looking well-groomed and well-dressed as a bother or as an opportunity? What about the condition of your work space or your office? In these seemingly personal matters, are you congruent to or divergent from the image of your company or organization?

If you feel a need to be different in these areas—to "march to your own drummer"—you may be making a mistake. This is not about freedom versus conformity. It's really about self-interest in the simplest and most positive sense. When Richard Nixon wore a gray suit for his debate, maybe he saw it as a chance to show that he could wear whatever color he wanted. Maybe someone told him to wear a dark-colored suit that would show up better on TV, but he asserted his right to be different and choose his own clothes. But no one in the audience was thinking in those terms. Instead, they simply responded negatively to the way Richard Nixon looked. People who couldn't see him—those who were listening to the debate on the radio—liked what Nixon had to say. But for those who could see him, his message was canceled out by his appearance. It was that simple.

Now let's look at the same issue from the opposite angle. When people are speaking to you, do you listen with full attention or are you distracted by their appearance, their phrasings, or other details? Is listening a matter of waiting for the other person to stop so that you can start talking, or is it a skill that you genuinely want to develop? It's amazing how rare good listeners are, and by becoming one of those rare people, you can take a big step toward making yourself truly unforgettable.

How do you react when someone says something that you disagree with? Do you find certain topics or certain people immediately irritating? We all have our hot buttons, but here again, an important aspect of class is to be in control and to accept responsibility. When someone says something that seems totally off-the-wall, he or she may indeed be an uninformed person. But it's not your responsibility to inform the world of that. Your responsibility is to respond with coolness, calm, and control—in a word, with *class.*

The title of Dale Carnegie's most famous book is *How to Win Friends and Influence People.* The title is known around the world, and its simplicity is one of its strengths—but to really understand that title, we need to look closely at one word. Surprisingly, that word is *and.* In ordinary conversation, *and* is just a linking word, a conjunction. But here those three letters have a more important function. *And* in the title of Dale Carnegie's book really means "in order to." The two parts of the title don't just coexist. One part grows from the other. It's not just a matter of making friends *and* influencing people. Making friends *allows* you to influence people. Making friends *gives you the power* to influence people. In the fewest possible words, *gaining affection confers respect.*

Regarding this, let's say it one final time: it's not rocket science! It's simple. Not necessarily easy, but definitely uncomplicated. Let's conclude this chapter with a number of principles—not just to bear in mind, but to *act upon,* starting today.

First, as part of your commitment to yourself as a class act and an unforgettable person, don't criticize, condemn, or complain. Period. Why not? Well, do you enjoy listening to other people's complaints? Does hearing someone condemn someone else endear you to that person? Does hearing a list of criticisms from someone incline you to be positively influenced by the person? I think the answers to these questions are self-explanatory.

Instead of criticizing or complaining, create in yourself feelings of appreciation and gratitude. Don't do this because you want to be a Pollyanna. Do it out of *positive self-interest.* Once again, how do you feel around people who are positive and appreciative? The chances are, those are the kinds of people you'll want for your friends. And as Dale Carnegie showed, friends are the people who influence us. We generally want to forget about people who are habitually negative, but genuinely positive people are not just memorable—they're literally unforgettable.

What's the best way to show appreciation, gratitude, optimism, and other positive feelings? Once again, what you say can be canceled out by how you look—so *smile*! What could be simpler? There's really no need to go deeply into the benefits of smiling, but it's interesting to note what research has shown. Smiling—that is, flexing the muscles of the face—stimulates the production of certain neurochemicals in the brain that are associated with feelings of pleasure and well-being. At the most basic biological level, smiling is good for you.

And laughing may be even better than smiling. More than twenty years ago, Norman Cousins wrote a bestselling book describing how he watched movie comedies to deal with a serious illness. Since then, there have been many studies of the physical and emotional effects of laughter. One interesting study tracked the frequency with which people laugh at various stages of life. At the age of three, we're really laughing a lot—hundreds of times a day. From then on, however, there's a gradual lessening of laughter over many years. But then something interesting happens. Some people start laughing more, and others stop laughing altogether.

Part of this may reflect genetics, but remember, an essential aspect of class is taking 100 percent responsibility. It may be that it's simply "natural" to become unhappier as we grow older. But that doesn't mean you have to let it happen. It may also be natural to become physically weaker and to gain weight, but millions of people have made it a priority to resist that process. You can make a commitment to keep your emotions positive just as you can to keep your body healthy. But *commitment* is a key word. It doesn't happen by itself. It doesn't happen easily. As we've discussed, class in general doesn't happen easily. You just have to make it look as if it does!

In the next chapter and those that follow, we'll be looking at specific aspects of class—what they are, how you can develop them, and how they can benefit you and those around you. But the concept of total responsibility that we've introduced here in chapter 2 is the foundation on which everything else is built.

You have the power to be a class act. You have what it takes to be a truly unforgettable person.

CHAPTER THREE

Inspiration, Not Imitation

Talk to anyone who's working in human resources at a major corporation and you'll hear a paradoxical message. The good news is, people applying for managerial positions are better qualified than ever. They have glowing academic records, often including degrees in business or accounting. They have solid work experience, with sincere letters of recommendation from their supervisors. They present themselves effectively in interviews, with excellent knowledge of the company they hope to work for, and of the economy as a whole.

The bad news is, everyone looks great on paper and in interviews, but everyone also looks exactly the same. People have figured out how to present themselves as competent, qualified managers who won't make waves and who won't make mistakes—but nobody is able to say, "I've got ideas that are really new and different!" People are afraid to present themselves as innovators, and consequently innovation itself has become a lost art.

This is a problem for American business. But it's also a golden opportunity for anyone who values originality and knows how to put it to work. You can instantly set yourself apart from the crowd by focusing on what you'll do right instead of what you won't do wrong. To do that, you'll need insight about your strengths and weaknesses, and intelligence about how to maximize your contribution. But most of all you'll need inspiration—the power to create energy and excitement by what you say, how you look, and above all, what you do. Those are some of the topics we'll be talking about in this chapter.

As a first step toward making yourself unforgettable to others, consider how you see yourself in your own eyes. Image is built upon self-perception. If your self-perception is out of sync with the way you want to be perceived, you will have a hard time making a positive impression—especially if you're not even fully aware of the problem. This happens to many people. For some reason, we tend to think less of ourselves than we'd like. We also tend to have a lower opinion of ourselves than other people have of us.

It may be that you don't want to seem egotistical or that you don't want to elevate your self-image at the expense of others, but putting yourself down is definitely not a good way to get ahead. So right now, recognize that you deserve to think of yourself in a far better light than you've gotten used to. This will not only make you feel more confident and deserving of success, but it will probably also bring you a lot closer to the truth of your image in the world.

Until you stop selling yourself short, you shouldn't be surprised if the world does the same thing. But the purpose of this book, and of this chapter in particular, is to help you set yourself apart from other people.

Here's a good way to start moving in that direction. We're going to look at your most significant achievements in three different areas of your life: your work and career; your education; and your relationships with family and friends. We're going to look at the things you've done right—and if you haven't done some of them as right as you would like, these are also the areas in which you will commit yourself to doing better. These are things you deserve to be proud of—and if you're not proud now, you have a great opportunity to change that.

And remember, focusing on your achievements—past, present, and future—doesn't mean you're being egotistical or self-centered. It's giving yourself credit where credit is due, and just being able to do that will immediately set you apart from the crowd.

WORK AND CAREER

Maybe your present livelihood is exactly what you always wanted to do—or you may be in a job or industry that you never expected to enter. You may be happy about what you're doing, or you may be disappointed. But for the time being, let's put all that aside. Without addressing any of the complexities of where you work or why you work there, try to identify the single best accomplishment of your career. It can be something you did for your employer, or something you did for yourself, or something you did to help one of your colleagues.

To understand this, imagine that you're Bill Gates, one of the wealthiest people in the world. Take a stroll through your forty-eight-thousand-square-foot home near Seattle, and ponder the question we've just been discussing. What's the best thing you've done in your work and career? In business decision-making, certainly one of your highlights was licensing your computer operating system to IBM for almost no money, provided you could retain the right to license the system to other computer manufacturers as well. IBM was happy to agree because, after all, nobody would possibly want to compete with the most powerful company in the world, right? With that one decision, your system and your company became dominant throughout the world, and you, Bill Gates, were on your way to a net worth of more than $60 billion.

Or maybe you'd like to look at your greatest career achievement from a different angle. Instead of focusing on the decision that helped you make so much money, maybe you'd like to look at the decision to give so much of it away. After all, no other person in history has become a philanthropist on the scale of Bill Gates. Nations in Africa and Asia are receiving billions of dollars in medical and educational support. This may not be as well publicized as your big house on Lake Washington with its digitalized works of art, but it's certainly something to be proud of.

Determining your greatest career achievement is a personal decision. It can be something obvious or something subtle. But it should make you proud of yourself when you think of it. So take a moment, then make your choice.

YOUR EDUCATION

Our next achievement category concerns your education, and your definition of education here should be broad. Did you get straight A's all through school? If so, that's great and it's certainly something to be proud of. But, without taking anything away from being on the honor role, it won't really set you apart from the crowd. As the admissions officer of any top university will tell you, they could fill every spot in every class with students who had perfect 4.0 averages in high school. Similarly, every applicant to leading MBA schools has a cum laude or a dean's-list undergraduate record. So instead of depending on the standard objective measures of educational success, think about what you know that perhaps nobody else does.

What have you really learned to do, whether it's writing or painting or sewing or working on your car? How did you acquire this skill? Did you learn it from someone else, or did you read about it, or is it something that you picked up entirely on your own? Is it something that came easily to you, or did it require consistent work and study? An educational achievement here means anything that you have learned really well—and that maybe no one else knows to the same high degree. What have you learned that you can be truly proud of? Think about that now.

YOUR CLOSEST RELATIONSHIPS

Now let's turn to an area of your life that you would probably say is the most important of all. Strangely, it's also the one that tends to get lost in the struggle to achieve our goals.

If you ask people what they want to do with their lives, you can expect to get all sorts of different answers. But if you ask them why—especially if there are children in their lives—you will almost always get a variation of the same answer: "I'm not doing it for myself. I'm doing it for my family. I'm doing it for the people who are closest to me and who are depending on me."

You can hear people in their twenties making statements like that, and you can also hear it from people in their sixties. A tremendous amount of emotion and effort are directed toward our human relationships, but when do we stop to recognize the payoff for all of this? When do we really take time to acknowledge what we have achieved for and with the people in our lives? That's what I'd like you to do right now.

What is is your greatest achievement in your relationships with other people, whether it's family or close friends? When was there a moment that, when you look back on it, you can say, "This is what makes it all worthwhile"? It can be a marriage or a graduation or something much less public. But it should be an occasion that makes you feel good about yourself and what you've achieved in a human relationship.

Now, as you look back on your achievements in your work, in your education, and in your relationships with others, you'll have found some genuine reasons to feel good about yourself. Don't forget that feeling, and don't forget the moments in time that connect you with it. You can use these memories as anchors to prevent your drifting away from a sense of positive identity. That's the kind of drift that can happen all too easily in a fast-paced, competitive world. So resist that trend. By doing so, you'll take a big step toward becoming unforgettable to everyone you meet. Even more important, you'll become unforgettable to yourself.

SETTING YOURSELF APART

We've seen how, in today's business marketplace, being well qualified is not enough, especially if your good qualifications are the same as everyone else's. For the rest of this chapter, we'll be looking at ways you can set yourself apart. We'll see how you can show that you're valuable—as a manager, as a colleague, and even as a friend. We'll also see how to be original, so that you're as good or better than the competition, and you're different in some positive ways. By accomplishing those two objectives, you'll definitely have gone a long way toward making yourself unforgettable.

Business leadership is based on two elements: vision and technical competence. Top people in a given industry always embody at least one of those two elements. Sometimes, but rarely, they embody both of them. Simply put, vision is the ability to see what other people don't. It's a Ford executive named Lee Iacocca realizing that a market existed for an automobile that was both a racing car and a street vehicle—and coming up with the Mustang. It's Steven Jobs realizing that computers needed to be sold in a single box, like a television sets, instead of piece by piece.

About one hundred years ago, Walter Chrysler was a plant manager for a locomotive company. Then he decided to go into the car business, which was a hot new industry at the time. The trouble was, Walter Chrysler didn't know a lot about cars, except that they were beginning to outnumber horses on the public roadways. To remedy this problem, Chrysler bought one of the Model T Fords that were becoming so popular. To learn how it worked, he took it apart and put it back together. Then, just to be sure he understood everything, he repeated this. Then, to be absolutely certain he knew what made a car work, he took it apart and put it together forty-eight more times, for a grand total of fifty. By the time he was finished, Chrysler not only had a vision of thousands of cars on American highways, he also had the mechanical details of those cars engraved in his consciousness.

Perhaps you've seen the play called *The Music Man*. It's about a fast-talking man who arrives in a small town with the intention of hugely upgrading a marching band. However, he can't play any instruments, doesn't know how to lead a band, and doesn't really have any musical skills whatsoever.

The Music Man is a comedy, but it's not totally unrealistic. Some managers in the computer industry don't know how to format a document. Some automobile executives could not change a tire. There was once even a vice president who couldn't spell *potato.* It's not a good idea to lack the fundamental technical skills of your industry, and it's really not a good idea to get caught lacking them. So let's see what you can do to avoid those problems.

The first step is to ask yourself some revealing questions. If you find yourself answering no to these questions, you need to do some work in this area right away. And even if most of your answers are affirmative, you can use these questions as guideposts. They can suggest new steps for enhancing yourself in these areas. They can call your attention to people you know who are especially competent or otherwise impressive—people whom you can learn from, people you might like to know better. In general, the questions we'll be asking can help you to do more.

So here are some items to think about regarding technical competence:

Are your ideas and opinions readily accepted? Or are your suggestions frequently challenged and turned down, often because they're considered impractical?

To what degree do others call upon your expertise? Are you often asked to make decisions involving technical matters? Or do people seem to lack confidence in your know-how?

Do you keep up with new developments in your business and industry? Or are you inclined to keep doing things the way you've always done them?

Give those questions some thought. As you do so, here are some specific actions you can take for elevating your technical competence, and also for making sure that it gets recognized.

Make sure that you read the trade journals and major Internet sites for your business or industry. Learn the names and titles of the executives at major companies. Be able to discuss new products and services from an operational perspective. Make sure you're comfortable using the industry buzzwords and jargon that the experts use to recognize each other. Most important, really make an effort to learn the technical side of your business. If you can do that, you'll distinguish yourself from the vast majority of people occupying managerial positions today. It's definitely worth the effort. By being technically competent, you'll be perceived as hugely valuable—and as technical competence becomes rarer, you'll also be seen as a total and unforgettable original.

DO YOU HAVE A FAILURE TO COMMUNICATE?

We've seen how you can make yourself stand out by mastering the nuts-and-bolts issues in your industry. As a corollary to that, you'll also need to communicate your understanding to the people you work with. We've all known people who were masters in their chosen field, but who had yet to achieve mastery in sharing what they knew.

The strange thing is, people who are less than great communicators often don't realize that they have this problem. An engineer can fill up a blackboard with diagrams and numbers, and he'll expect all his listeners to know exactly what it all means. Actually, it might mean nothing to anybody. It might be totally unintelligible, and even worse, no one will admit that. So right now, let's focus on assessing your ability to communicate, and also on enhancing that ability. After all, being an original thinker is not worth much if no one understands what you're thinking. If that's the case, you might be unforgettable, but it won't be for the reasons you want!

Here are some questions and ideas to help with this.

Do you enjoy being in the company of people you work with?

This can be a good way of knowing whether they enjoy being with you. The late Marlon Brando was once asked if he considered himself the best actor in Hollywood. That was a treacherous question, but Brando answered it in a creative way. He said, "It doesn't matter whether I'm the best actor. I'm the best-positioned actor. People know me, and they want me around. I make life interesting for the people around me. It's fun for me and it's fun for them. I'm not always a nice guy, but I'm never the same guy twice. That's why studios want to put me in movies, and that's why the public wants to see me there." Are you like Brando in this respect? Do you get together with your colleagues even when you don't have to? If the answer is yes, you're on the right track. If the answer is no, ask yourself, whom would you rather be with? Then think about how you can make a career move in that direction.

Do you communicate with your colleagues even when it's not strictly necessary—by phone, e-mail, or in person? Or are you more comfortable being on your own? There probably has never been a person who was more challenged in this area than Howard Hughes. He was undeniably a technical expert, and he was certainly unforgettable. He could design an airplane, fly it, and also direct a movie about it. But it was very, very difficult for him to connect personally with his employees. Hughes once interviewed a candidate for an engineering job. At the close of the interview, Hughes said he didn't think the man was suited to be an engineer, but another job was available that might be interesting. The pay was the same as for an engineer, and this job was actually a lot simpler. All the candidate had to do was to sit in a hotel suite from nine till five o'clock each day—but if the telephone ever rang, he had to answer it on the first ring. There was nothing else to it. No further information would be given, and no questions could be asked. It was just a matter of answering the telephone on the first ring. The man took the job and spent three workweeks in the hotel room. The telephone never rang, and he couldn't take it anymore. He quit the job.

This may sound like an over-the-top example, but it's

essentially what always happens when you give an assignment without communicating the purpose and the rationale behind it. That purpose may be clear to you, but that's just the start. You must then make it clear to others. If you can't do that, you'd better have as much money as Howard Hughes, because your career prospects may be severely limited.

A few more points:

If you have a difference of opinion with someone, do you feel you always need to win? If so, choose your words carefully. How you express yourself will be remembered long after what you said is forgotten.

If someone is the target of another person's anger, do you instinctively take one person's side? Don't rush to judgment even if others do. There are two sides to any dispute, and there's also the wise option of not getting involved if you don't have to.

Above all, making yourself stand out as a manager or an employee means walking a fine line. It's great to be sociable—but it's not great to be sociable and nothing more. It's good to circulate within the organizational culture, but it's not good to hang around the watercooler.

"You really like me!"

When the actress Sally Field spoke those words as she accepted an Academy Award, she was touching upon an issue that many people share. Research shows that three things go through people's minds when meeting someone for the first time. First, they make an assessment of the newcomer's intelligence and education. Is this someone who's in my ballpark in knowledge of the world, or are we on radically different levels? Is this someone who's significantly below me intellectually, or am I intimidated by this total Einstein?

As a class act, it's best not to be perceived at either extreme of the spectrum. Most people are uncomfortable with geniuses, and they're definitely turned off by intellectual posers. They're also turned off by airheads—so act accordingly.

The second judgment we make about new acquaintances

concerns finances. Is this person rich or the opposite? Do you use the credit card to buy groceries, or do you own the credit-card company?

Again, there's not much benefit in being seen at either extreme. As with great intelligence, it's hard for us to identify with great wealth. And being in the presence of financial stress can actually be frightening to many people. So be aware that money questions are going through the minds of new acquaintances, and try not to let money become a separation point.

So early on, people assess whether someone new is smart, and whether he or she is rich. But the third assessment is definitely the most important, and it's a quality we touched on toward the end of the previous chapter. The third thing people wonder about is whether they can be friends with you. Not whether you can help them get ahead, not whether you would win or lose at golf, but whether you could be their friend. Human beings want that more than anything else from a new acquaintance—and Dale Carnegie was one of the first people to make that clear.

It's not easy to define exactly what will ignite friendship in another person. But the ability to light that spark is the single most important element in making yourself stand out from the crowd of people who pass through our lives. In four short principles—one of them is only a single word long—Dale Carnegie came closer than anyone else to revealing the secret of friendship, which is literally the secret of success. Our topic in this chapter has been making yourself stand out as an inspired original, and these points will certainly help you do that. But I strongly suggest you keep them in mind as the foundation of everything you'll hear in these chapters. Remember: friendship is what human beings want most, and this is how to give it to them:

First, take a genuine interest in other people. *Genuine* is the key word. Don't fake it. Train yourself to actually become interested in other people's lives. You yourself may be totally fascinating, but that doesn't mean you're the only one who's totally fascinating. Show people you understand that.

Second, remember that a person's name is, to that person, the most important word in any language. Focus on remembering someone's name as soon as you meet the person. Use the name in your conversation so that you don't forget.

Third, make the other person feel important—and do it sincerely. Once again, sincerity is the important thing. An ancient proverb says, "Wisdom is the power to learn something from everyone." If you want to be wise, if you want to be unforgettable, if you want to be a class act, find the important thing that you can learn from only one person—the person you're talking with right now.

Fourth and last is a single-sentence principle: *smile.* What could be simpler? Smile. In fact, smile right now!

CHAPTER FOUR
Honesty with Honor

We live in a society that values communication skills highly. We've also become quite sophisticated about how those skills can express themselves. We like people who are able to express themselves well, but we also realize that there's more than one way to do that.

In chapter 1 we saw how President Kennedy was able to make a favorable impression in his debate with Richard Nixon. But Ronald Reagan and Barack Obama were equally effective in their own debates, although they had completely different styles. They did have one thing in common: each of them was unforgettable.

In light of this, is it possible to draw any general conclusions about what good communicating involves? Certain principles definitely underlie all effective communication, but the number of ways those principles can be applied is almost infinite. In fact, there are just about as many ways to apply the principles as there are people to apply them. So pay attention. By the end of this chapter you'll know just what style of communication will make *you* an unforgettable class act.

TO TELL THE TRUTH

The foundation of communicating effectively can be expressed in one word: *honesty.* That means *telling the truth.* For our purposes here, we're going to take it for granted that you accept this premise. Being a class act doesn't include doing anything deceptive. Making yourself unforgettable does not involve shaving the edges off the truth. But you are going to see that there are different ways of honestly expressing yourself—which is not only for your benefit, but also for the benefit of your listeners.

Sometimes, for example, it will be best to take the shortest and quickest route to the truth. Chicken Little did not beat around the bush! He came right out and said, "The sky is falling!" It was a real emergency, or at least he felt it was, and he wanted to convey the essential information in the least possible time. Even if it's not an emergency, you need to speak very directly to some people. That's what they want, and that's what they need.

The word we'll use to indicate this direct form of communication is *frankness.* Generally speaking, frankness is something most Americans say they appreciate. "Just the facts, ma'am"—that's the way we like it. Or so we say.

Let's look quickly at an example of the value of frank communication—and the problems that can arise in its absence.

Janice is the director of marketing at an East Coast home-products company. One morning she was unexpectedly summoned to a meeting with her supervisor and the chief operating officer of the firm. The purpose of the meeting was to discuss ways of improving communication. But to Janice's surprise, it seemed that most of the discussion had already taken place without her. She was told that a number of her responsibilities would now be outsourced to an independent contractor.

Janice had been with the company for ten years. She felt blindsided. She understood that reorganizations are sometimes necessary, but why hadn't she been part of the initial discussions?

What's more, why had she been told that she was going to be part of a discussion, only to find out that it had already happened?

Actually, the reason was simple. Janice's supervisors felt that if they approached her frankly about what was in the works, she would have become angry. Maybe they were right. But she became even angrier when she was excluded from the deliberations.

What took place here was a form of dishonesty. In a larger sense, it was an absence of class. Class, you'll remember, is based on taking full responsibility for your ideas and actions. What happened here was the opposite of taking responsibility. It was trying to spread responsibility around so that nobody had to own up to it—not even the senior managers of the company. Rather than striving to make yourself unforgettable, it was trying to become invisible.

Even senior executives often try to avoid direct discussions with the people who will be affected by a decision. Instead of going directly to the manager in question, executives may try to float trial balloons with others at the company to gauge reaction and get support. That, however, only stirs rumors, erodes teamwork, and fundamentally undermines communication.

If Janice had known she was going to meet with this kind of dishonesty, what could she have done? What was the class act she could have undertaken to protect her interests?

Ideally, Janice would have developed such a trusting relationship with her supervisors that frank communication would not have frightened them. True, if they were better executives, they would not have been frightened in the first place, but not all are as competent as they should be. Secondly, if Janice suspected that changes were about to be made, she herself could have spoken out frankly even when others wouldn't. "Is there something I need to be aware of?" would have been a good way to put it. Sometimes you have to insert yourself into the communications. This isn't being pushy or insubordinate. It's just making sure your interests aren't overlooked, especially for insignificant reasons. It's literally making yourself unforgettable in a practical sense.

Even after a decision is imposed on you as a manager, you shouldn't necessarily just give in to it. "If a manager senses decisions are being made about him behind his back, it's all right to ask, 'Is there something I'm doing that made you reluctant to come to me? And if there is, I'd like to deal with it now so that I can fully participate in what we're doing here.'" Speaking frankly in that way provides an opening for a conversation—or forces an opening, if that's what's necessary.

Regarding frankness, there is one other thing to be aware of. Being frank almost always includes some risk. If you intend to speak frankly and you feel there's no risk attached, you're probably not really speaking frankly. Think of fables such as "The Emperor's New Clothes," in which a young boy risks his life by telling the truth in a direct manner. It takes guts to be frank. It takes class. But when you feel that honesty must be communicated very directly, there really is no choice.

WINNING THEIR HEARTS AND MINDS

Your status as a class act meets its greatest challenges—and also its greatest opportunities—when you need to gain the cooperation of others. This is especially true when they have ideas or opinions different from your own. Situations such as that require a careful balance of skills. It may take personal strength just to confront the situation. On the surface, it often seems easier to pretend differences don't exist than to initiate action to work for a mutually agreeable solution. Sensitivity is required to draw out another person's true objectives through questioning and careful, nonjudgmental listening.

Many of the principles Dale Carnegie writes about in *How to Win Friends and Influence People* apply directly to communication.

Keep the following points in mind:

- *To get the best of an argument—avoid it.*
- *Show respect for the other person's opinion. Never tell a person he or she is wrong.*
- *If you are wrong, admit it quickly, emphatically.*
- *Begin in a friendly way. Get the other person saying "yes" immediately.*
- *Let the other person do a great deal of the talking.*
- *Let the other person feel the idea is his or hers.*
- *Speak softly.*
- *Smile appropriately.*
- *If a confrontation can't be avoided, don't feel you have to get an unconditional surrender. Always give the other person an opening for an honorable retreat.*

RESOLVING CONFLICT

This intelligent approach to resolving conflicts is not as easy as it may sound. Sometimes you may not feel calm, rational, or open-minded. The psychologist William James wrote, "Action seems to follow feeling, but really action and feeling go together; and by regulating the action, which is under the more direct control of the will, we can indirectly regulate the feeling."

In other words, when you adopt the actions of a calm, rational person, you become calm and rational. When you act open-minded, your mind actually opens up. And almost magically, the person with whom you are interacting mirrors those behaviors and adopts the same feelings.

DIPLOMACY

Sometimes people who don't express themselves well will try to turn this into a virtue. "I may not be very good with words," they'll say, "but at least you know where I'm coming from. At least I'm honest."

What are the foundations of a statement like that? First, there's the implication that people who *are* good with words are inherently suspect of dishonesty. Such an idea is wrongheaded. Honesty can take many different forms. Not everyone wants to be spoken to in a blunt way. Not everyone wants to speak bluntly either.

Unforgettable communicators are people who know what they have to say, but they are also aware of the needs of the people who have to listen to them. Let's take a look at what that involves, step by step.

DIPLOMACY IN ACTION

Before anything else, it's important to establish rapport. Frank conversations may be confrontational—hopefully in a positive way—but diplomatic communication should always take place in an atmosphere of civility. There may be much more going on beneath the surface, as there was between Steve and Ben, but that doesn't need to be made explicit. This doesn't mean you're being dishonest. It just means you're being diplomatic.

Next, bring up the problem in a calm and composed manner. A judgmental or accusing tone is almost never useful. It just gives people an excuse to get their defenses up and to respond in a personal way. If you're angry enough, you may be tempted to run down the other person's accomplishments and tell them how worthless he or she is—but once again, this will just invite a response in kind. Although he had caught Ben in a clear case of dishonesty and insubordination, Steve found a way to mention what a good job Ben had done in his work—which was actually the truth.

Be sure to let the other person tell his or her side of the story. Ben did not have much to say in this regard, but Steve clearly offered him an opportunity. Make sure you listen respectfully to whatever is said. Once again, avoid argument or confrontation.

Make constructive suggestions. Be sure these are expressed in a way that doesn't put people down or humiliate them. Emphasize *what* rather than *who.* Base the discussion on the wrongful action, not the character flaws of the person who did it. Encourage positive change through effective questioning and active listening. Then arrange a nonthreatening follow-up both to measure progress and make any further corrections.

End the interview by reassuring the employee of his or her worth to the organization. If you've truly been a class act, the person will leave the interview motivated to follow the suggestions that have been made. This will not be because of fear, but because he or she sees a positive future with you and with the organization.

Here's one last tactic to keep in mind. Some people may find it easy; others may find it difficult. *Don't raise your voice.* Once the decibels rise above a certain level in an encounter between two people, nothing positive can come from it. Things may definitely happen when people are yelling at each other, but they won't be good things. One of the worst things anyone can say about a manager is that he or she is a "screamer."

Teddy Roosevelt said, "Speak softly and carry a big stick." And if you don't have a big stick, speak softly anyway.

DISCIPLINE: THE FINAL INGREDIENT

After more than thirty-five years as an insurance executive in Chicago, Jim was ready to retire. He and his wife, Joyce, had purchased a home in Florida, and they were definitely looking forward to missing their first Midwestern winter. They were even excited about making the long drive down to Florida. There was no hurry, and they could take as long as they wanted to get to their new home.

As things turned out, getting there took a little longer than they might have wanted. They were driving through northern Alabama at about ten in the morning when a loud noise came from under the car. It wasn't an explosion, but more like a metallic crash—and it was followed by a loud and continuous rattling. Whatever this was, it wasn't good. Jim immediately slowed the car to almost walking speed and pulled to the right lane of the highway. Luckily, an exit was only a few yards ahead, so at least they wouldn't be stuck on the shoulder of the interstate. Going as slowly as possible, Jim made his way up the exit ramp. The rattling was still going on, but slower now, in proportion to the speed of the car. Jim and Joyce didn't say a word, but just looked at each other. They had been through a lot over the years, but they hadn't expected retirement to be like this.

As Jim reached the top of the ramp, he was glad to see a service station up ahead. Still going as slowly as possible, he reached the station and turned off the engine.

There, Jim and Joyce met Norm, a man they would get to know quite well that day. Norm looked as if he hadn't changed his overalls since the Kennedy administration, but he obviously knew how to take care of a car. Although he was a large man, Norm immediately crawled under the chassis with the agility of a yard lizard.

"Well, look at that," he announced from beneath the car. "Must have been a length of tire chain lying in the road, because that's what you've got wrapped around the axle. Wrapped real tight, too—and it's gone and ripped a hole in the undercarriage."

Jim didn't like what he was hearing. He didn't know much about cars, but he sensed that an unpleasant few hours were about to begin. Meanwhile, Norm emerged from beneath the car and said, "What a mess."

Jim nodded. "Well, what's it going to take to fix it?"

Norm shook his head slowly, as if he'd just been asked to spell an extremely difficult word. "That's hard to say at this point. First we need to get that chain off the axle. I'll have to use a torch for that, and I'll have to be really careful with it, too. Then we'll see how much damage has been done to the underside of the car. There might be some welding involved. I just can't give you all the details at this point."

"I guess I can understand that," Jim said. "But what would you estimate it's going to cost?"

"Like I said, I can't give you all the details at this point." Then Norm was silent. He didn't need to say, "You don't have much choice, do you?" because that was already perfectly clear.

Before giving Norm the go-ahead to begin any work, Jim took his wife aside for a private conversation. "If this is what retirement is like, I'd just as soon go back to work."

Joyce smiled. "You may have to go back to work, because we could really get held up here." But then she added, "Let's try to look at it as a comedy instead of a tragedy. We're stuck here, so let's make the best of it. Things could be a lot worse. Just tell him to get started so we can get out of here ASAP."

Within a few minutes, Norm had the car in the service bay. While he was working, Jim and Joyce explored the area around the gas station. There was absolutely nothing to do. Another gas station was across the interstate, and that was about it. Then it started to rain. The trucks whizzed past on the highway creating wakes of spray. There was nothing to do but take refuge in the service bay where Norm was working on the car.

As he worked, Norm talked. He talked about his family, his dogs, his cars, his house, his roof, and his basement. But mostly he talked about football. He seemed able to recall every detail of every game ever played in the Southeastern Conference. Sometimes he would get so caught up in what he was saying that he stopped work to describe a crucial run or interception.

After several hours of this, Jim took Joyce aside again. "I feel like he's trying to go as slow as possible," Jim said. "He's trying to drag it out. He's not a mechanic. He's a holdup man."

Joyce was still reassuring. "Just think of it as a challenge. Someday we'll be laughing about this."

At close to five o'clock, Norm finally shut down his welding torch. The work had taken all day. "Well, that was a big job," he told Jim and Joyce. "But it gave us a chance to get to know each other, didn't it?"

"Yes, it really did," Jim answered, forcing a smile. "So what do we owe you?"

Norm thought for a moment, then casually waved his hand. "Aw, don't worry about it. I'll do it for free. But that game in 1974 was quite a contest . . ."

What Jim and Joyce experienced here was truly a chance to win friends and influence people, and they took full advantage of it. Although it wasn't easy, they turned a potential conflict into an opportunity for communication—not just in what was said, but in what was felt. As a result, getting their car fixed was not just free.

It was *unforgettable.* Making that happen is what class is all about.

CHAPTER FIVE

Listening: The Key Communication Skill

Of all the communications skills, effective listening can make the biggest difference in your relationships with others. Yet listening doesn't come naturally to most people. A certain amount of work is involved, especially when you're just learning how to become an effective listener.

Unfortunately, most people don't really listen with attention. They just try to keep quiet until it's their turn to speak. Maybe it's just human nature to feel as if you can just jump into a conversation and start talking, or at least *want* to do that. But this is one of the many areas in which class will call upon you to resist your initial impulses. So don't just react. Put yourself in control.

Because the ability to listen well is such a valuable skill, a significant amount of research has been devoted to understanding it. All sorts of metaphors and terminologies have been created to describe listening. But the core message of all these systems is the same: more is going on than just the understanding of words.

Sometimes good listening is as much about silence as it is about sounds. Good listeners give other people the chance to be quiet just as they also give them the chance to speak. Listening in the truest sense includes many nonverbal and nonaudible factors, such as body language, facial expressions, cultural assumptions, and the reactions of the speakers and the listeners to each other.

Obviously, the experience of listening varies from person to person. It also depends on the context: who's speaking to whom, what is the subject, and where is the conversation taking place? Listening to a police officer who has pulled you over in a traffic stop is different from listening to your eight-year-old daughter or your eighty-year-old father-in-law.

The categories listed below describe various levels of listening—from the least attentive to the most empathic and beneficial. As you read them through, think about their relevance to your own ability to listen. Be aware that, to make yourself unforgettable, you need to give people your full attention when they're speaking with you. It's the class thing to do!

"CHECKED-OUT" LISTENING (OR NOT REALLY LISTENING AT ALL)

You're sitting there with a vague awareness that somebody is talking to you, but that's about it. This is one step from outright ignoring the person. At times this minimal listening is the appropriate thing to do. If you're being harangued by someone who's just determined to give you a lecture for his or her own satisfaction, the best thing to do may be to just be there physically while you're mentally on vacation in Hawaii. But make sure this is a conscious and well-considered choice, not just an impolite reflex.

MINIMAL LISTENING

Checked-out listening is basically a one-way street. Someone is talking, and you're there but not really there. Your participation in the form of body language or verbal responses is basically zero. Minimal listening, however, replaces daydreaming with at least a certain amount of taking part in the conversation. You hear and reply to what's being said, although your responses are "prefabricated." You're telling the other person what you think he wants to hear to keep him comfortable. Unfortunately, this is often how we engage with children and elderly people. It is also common in business settings, when a supervisor is called upon to hear the concerns of a disgruntled employee. As a minimal listener, your intentions are good but your listening is still at a low level. Sometimes this will be obvious to the speaker. But because minimal listening usually occurs when there's a significant disparity between the chronological ages (or the corporate power) of the parties involved, the speakers will usually not register their disappointment out loud. Inwardly, however, they're sure to be thinking, "Will you *please* pay some real attention to what I'm saying!"

"I'M LISTENING TO YOU—BUT IT'S ALL ABOUT ME"

This is probably the most common level of listening between people who are not family members, longtime work colleagues, or close friends. Here you have an interest and perhaps some flexibility in respect to the words spoken and your reactions to them, but because you are not thinking objectively and purely, you are putting your own interpretation on what you are hearing—making the words fit what you expect or want them to fit. This is a type of projective listening like level two above, but you will not normally be aware that you are doing it until it is pointed out to you. This kind of listening is risky. It can leave you with a misguided interpretation of the actual facts and feelings. You're hearing and taking in information, but because you have a firmly opposed or differing viewpoint, you're not prepared to open the door to change. You hear the words of the speaker through the filter of your preexisting beliefs. Sometimes this will lead you to preemptively agree with the speaker, or it can also cause you to disagree. Quite often this expresses itself as a desire to tell your own story—which is probably a *much* better one, right?—as soon as the slightest opening presents itself. Once you become aware of this tendency, it's amazing how often you'll see it done—whether to you or by you.

"JUST THE FACTS" LISTENING

Especially among men, interpersonal communication can take the form of a pure and simple exchange of information. For women, a key purpose of any friendly conversation is the building of rapport and emotional connection. These differing expectations can lead to frequent misunderstandings. "Just the facts" is fine when the purpose of the communication is merely to convey what's what, but it's inadequate for dealing with feelings and motives. Yet connecting with feelings and motives is more often than not an essential part of why people want to speak with each other in the first place, the circumstances underneath the superficial words or sounds. This kind of listening can win a battle and lose a war; it can be an effective short-term tactic but not a good long-term strategy.

EMPATHIC LISTENING

This is getting closer to the complete package. It includes sensitivity to words, intonations, body language, and facial expressions. It also includes giving feedback. This requires you to have overall recognition of how the other person is feeling. You're able to *see* and *feel* the situation from someone else's point of view. You are frank and honest in expressing disagreement but at the same time striving for genuine understanding.

OPTIMAL LISTENING

More than even empathic listening, this includes an action-oriented component. You not only hear what's being said, but you're listening naturally leads you to suggest ideas for positive change on the part of the speaker. Or you may even offer to take action yourself on behalf of the speaker. This doesn't mean you're making decisions for the other person. It's just that optimal listening contains a strong element of helping someone understand their options. More than any of the preceding levels, in optimal listening the other person's interests are the focus.

A FEW COMMON MISTAKES

When misunderstandings occur, especially in the workplace, the problems are most often attributed to the speaker. We believe it's the speaker's responsibility to clearly convey whatever the message might be. But what about the listener? There's a basic misunderstanding here: we see speaking as a skill, without realizing that listening is also a skill that can be learned, improved, and perfected.

To see how this can take place, we'll begin with an overview of some common mistakes listeners make. Then we'll introduce some practical tools—not just for eliminating errors, but for making your listening as effective as it can possibly be.

Be aware that the traits discussed below aren't inherently good or bad. Sometimes they're "just what the doctor ordered." But as with all interpersonal behaviors, the key is to make conscious choices with full understanding of the effect those choices will have.

Rehearsing. This takes place when your attention is not on what you're hearing, but on what you plan to say as soon as you get an opening. You may look interested, but your thoughts are really on what to say next. Some people even plan a whole sequence of dialog: "I'll say this . . . then she'll say that . . . and then I'll say . . ."

Evaluating. If you prejudge a speaker as incompetent or uninteresting, you may be correct—but you may also be creating the very traits you criticize.

Playing "topper." This term, which was coined by the gifted Zig Ziglar, refers to the tendency to take everything you hear and refer it back to your own experience—which of course is much more interesting than the speaker's. The speaker tells you about a fish he caught, and you launch into a story about how you caught an even bigger fish. Most people who play topper can't even wait until the speaker finishes talking.

"Truth-telling." You are the great problem solver. You don't have to hear more than a few sentences before you begin to reveal your wisdom and insight. But is what you know at all congruent with what you're hearing? Few "truth-tellers" really care.

Faultfinding. You disagree just because you think it's fun to disagree, and you feel you can get away with it. As a corollary to this, you will do everything possible to avoid the appearance of being wrong.

Placating. This is the opposite of faultfinding, but it's really just another way of checking out. No matter what the speaker says, you give them a mildly positive response just to keep from genuinely connecting. "Right . . . Absolutely . . . I know . . . Incredible . . . Amazing . . . Really?"

Derailing. This means suddenly changing the subject. As with other listening errors, it's often done by people in a position of power over the speaker.

TOOLS FOR LISTENING

Listening effectively to others can be the most fundamental and powerful communication tool of all. When someone is willing to stop talking or thinking and begin truly listening to others, all of their interactions become easier, and communication problems are all but eliminated.

There are many tools and techniques for effective listening. But as with any tool, these are only effective when they're used correctly. Skilled listeners know how to adopt their responses to the speaker and the situation. Unskilled listeners create mismatches. They may be attempting to use the same tools as a good listener, but the application of the tools is out of sync with the circumstances.

The following is a selection of tools for good listening and for good communication in general. As you read through them, think not only about the tools themselves, but also about specific situations you have faced in which they might have been especially effective.

Make listening a conscious choice, not a passive reflex. If you're not prepared to give as much attention to the human being sitting across from you as you give to your computer screen or your iPod, just be honest about that. In a polite way, say, "This isn't really a good time to talk." Then suggest an alternative. If you do make the choice to listen, act on that choice to the fullest possible extent.

Put your expectations aside. Really listening to someone means hearing what is actually being said, rather than filtering it through what you expect or want to hear. You wouldn't try to listen to a person amid the distractions of a circus or a rodeo. By the same token, don't let your internal distractions—which can be much more compelling—get in the way of giving your full attention.

Ask questions. It's a good idea to ask three questions about the person who's speaking for every piece of information you offer about yourself. This is especially true when you're in a position of authority—for example, if you're a manager listening to the concerns of a team member. Once you become aware of this principle, you'll see how rarely it's actually followed. It's just as rare as other expressions of real class.

Maintain eye contact. Your understanding of what's being said is strongly affected by what you see as well as what you hear. Moreover, breaking eye contact with a speaker sends a negative or even a hostile message. Don't let this happen by accident.

Pay attention . . . and keep paying attention. Too often, people stop listening before they've heard the whole message. Sometimes speakers will hesitate to disclose what's really on their minds until the conversation is well under way. Be sure you don't check out too soon. It's a good idea to occasionally summarize what you have heard to test your understanding.

In the end, the secret to effective listening is nothing more than basic respect for another person. *You're listening, not judging. To the extent that you are nonjudgmental, people will be willing to talk candidly with you. And if they won't talk candidly, they might as well not talk at all.* If what you hear triggers an emotional response in you, accept full responsibility for your reactions. Remaining composed even when you feel your buttons are being pushed is a powerful expression of real class. This is especially important when people communicate something personal or painful. Respect is different from just feeling sorry for someone. It requires real understanding of others' feelings. Once this has happened, the foundation has been laid for you to share your own point of view.

CHAPTER SIX

Passionate Principle

In the 1990s, when the dot-com boom was at its peak, there seemed to be no limit to how much could be done—or how much money could be made—if you just had the nerve. And some people had a lot of nerve. More recently there was the same feeling about real estate, which seemed destined to keep rising in price forever. But "forever" turned out to be an unrealistically long time.

What happened? If people were smart enough to run huge companies, how could they make so many dumb mistakes? But some people weren't dumb. They were just greedy. But what happened—and why—is less important than what can be done to prevent such events in the future, especially as it effects your own life and career.

This raises issues on many levels. There are certainly legal issues, and there are also ethical concerns. The truth is, ethics involves a lot more than compliance with company policies and statutory laws. True, headlines are made when formal regulations are not obeyed—and for exactly those reasons, most organizations don't have problems with these issues. Instead, it's the "little things" that cause problems. Day-to-day, seemingly insignificant actions represent the largest area for ethics problems—and the greatest opportunity for improvement.

You may forget the little things you do, but they can have a significant impact on people around you, either positively or negatively. They can determine whether you're seen as an unforgettable class act, or something entirely different. You are always setting an example, whether you intend to or not. So what messages are you sending by your actions, words, and attitudes? Ask yourself, for example, whether you've done any of the following:

- Conducted personal business on company time?
- Used or taken company resources for personal purposes?
- Called in sick when you weren't sick?
- Used an ethnically offensive term when referring to another person?
- Told or passed along an ethnically or sexually oriented joke?
- Engaged in negative gossip, or spread rumors about someone?
- Bad-mouthed the company or someone in it to coworkers?
- Passed along information that had been shared in confidence?
- Failed to admit to or correct a mistake?
- Knowingly violated company rules or procedures?
- Failed to follow through on something you said you would do?
- Withheld information that others needed?
- Fudged on a time sheet, invoice, or expense account?
- Knowingly delivered second-rate goods or services?
- Been less than honest to make a sale
- Accepted an inappropriate gift or gratuity?
- Taken or accepted credit for something that someone else did?
- Knowingly let someone else make a mistake and get into trouble?

That's quite a long list! But these and other seemingly minor actions reflect who you are and what you stand for. When it comes to ethics and integrity, everything is important—especially "the small stuff."

ETHICS IS GETTING ATTENTION

Dov Seidman is the author of a book with a provocative title: *HOW: Why HOW We Do Anything Means Everything . . . in Business (and in Life)*. As Seidman explains on his website—howsmatter.com—the thesis of his book is that success is no longer only a matter of what we do or how much money we make by doing it. The means by which we get results are inseparable from the value of the results themselves.

Certainly this has always been true; the idea that the end can't be separated from the means is hardly new. But Seidman feels that the revolution in communications and high technology has changed the game. It's become much harder for an individual or a company to sustain a competitive advantage based simply on a product or service. Technology has made it easy to clone or improve whatever is being offered. As a result, relationships and reputation are becoming much more important.

As Seidman puts it:

> *In a connected world, individuals and organizations that make the strongest connections win. In the past, our products and services—our whats—were our keys to success. Today, whats have become commodities, easily duplicated or reverse engineered. Sustainable advantage and enduring success—for both companies and the people who work for them—now lie in the realm of how.*
>
> *Today, how we behave and interact with others is the ultimate differentiator. The qualities that most once thought of as "soft"—integrity, passion, humility, and truth—have become the hard currency of business success and the most powerful drivers of reputation and profitability.*

SITUATIONAL ETHICS

Let's look at some imaginary situations that can come up in a variety of settings. Use your imagination to put yourself into the situation that I describe, then choose one of the three hypothetical solutions. You'll probably recognize the ethically correct option right away, but be honest with yourself about the path that you would really take. If it's not the most ethical one, don't get down on yourself, but use this information as a signpost indicating the direction you really need to go.

Here's the first scenario:

A large nonprofit organization is considering making a donation to a school for children with special needs. You've been hired to evaluate the school's finances.

Most of the children's families are eligible for financial assistance from the state. You suspect some of the families are understating their household incomes so they can receive more aid. Your own inquiries show that one family is underreporting its income. As a result, their child's financial assistance package has been increased by almost 50 percent.

You know that this family's child would not be able to receive the services she's getting from the school without some financial assistance. You also know the child is benefiting physically and psychologically from the services she's receiving.

What would you do? Would you do nothing—because the child's welfare outweighs the school's need to know the truth about the family's income, which would still be low even if it were accurately reported? Besides, it's technically the state's responsibility to verify incomes for the financial assistance book.

Would you talk to the school administrator about the situation? Actually, you have reason to suspect that the administrator may already know about it. Might bringing this out into the open put the administrator in a dangerous situation along with the family?

Or would you contact an attorney or regulatory agency based on your suspicion of fraud?

Think about it for a moment. Remember, this is just an exercise. You're not going to be graded on your answer. Just try to be honest about the option you would choose.

Here's the next hypothetical setting:

As a manager in the marketing department of your company, you're familiar with the technical side of computer and Internet usage. The president of your company believes some employees are spending too much time on the Internet doing tasks not related to work. He asks you to start monitoring their Internet usage without their knowledge. You could easily do this from a technological standpoint, but you're not sure of the principles involved.

What would you do?

Would you start monitoring employees' e-mail and Web usage, as the president has asked?

Would you first suggest to the president that an acceptable Internet-use policy be developed and distributed throughout the company?

Or would you informally talk to a number of your coworkers and tell them about the president's concerns?

Now the third case history:

You're in graduate school at a major research university, pursuing your Ph.D. in chemistry. You've completed a series of experiments for your dissertation. Some of the data you've gathered in these experiments supports the theory you're trying to prove, while some does the opposite.

Your academic book requires you to publish a paper based on your research in a professional scientific journal. If you write and publish the paper focusing solely on the good data you've gathered in your experiments, you'll be well on your way to securing your degree. You'll also be likely to get additional funding.

On the other hand, if you publish a paper highlighting all your data—both positive and negative—you'll be taking a major risk. The organization paying for your research might be disappointed and cut off your funds.

Would you write and publish a paper highlighting all the data?

Would you write a paper featuring only the data that supports your research?

Or would you restructure your research project from the ground up, based on the new information you've gained?

The next case history:

You're an assistant in a graphic design firm. In your work you oversee the creation of annual reports and other documents. Usually you write the documents, collaborate with a designer to lay them out, then work with an outside printer to get the documents printed in large quantities.

When your latest brochure is about to come back from the printer, you spot an error in a headline on the third page.

Would you call the mistake to your supervisor's attention, even though it's relatively minor in the grand scheme of things and probably won't have any impact on the overall message the brochure is trying to communicate?

Or, in the interest of saving money and time, would you let the mistake go and distribute all the copies of the brochure?

Or would you speak to the graphic artist, who should probably have caught the mistake during production, and ask what went wrong and why? Would you be prepared to tell your supervisor about the graphic artist's mistake if the supervisor asked about it?

And the last scenario:

You're applying for a new job as a senior editor at a major news magazine. You're currently a staff writer at another publication, but due to layoffs you've been performing many editorial duties for almost a year now. You want your résumé to be taken seriously for the new position.

How would you describe yourself on your résumé?

Would you use the title *editor*? Because you've been performing the duties of an editor for at least a year, and it would be selling yourself short not to make that clear.

Or would you use your official title *staff writer* on your résumé, even though it doesn't accurately reflect the database skills you perform each day?

Or would you invent a new job title that better describes what you do each day? It wouldn't be your official title, but it would deliver the message you need to convey.

The situations we've just looked at would not make headlines and would not be reported on the evening news. But they're the type of ethical problems people face every day. They're the kinds of questions you need to answer to be an ethical manager and a principled human being.

You may be faced with someone proposing an action that you believe is not ethical. That someone may be above you in the company hierarchy. How would you respond? Would you "go along to get along"—or maybe even "go along to get ahead"?

That's exactly what many people do. Some of them *do* get ahead. Some of them also lose their jobs or even go to prison. So fight the temptation to compromise your ethics. Take a stand. If "just say no" seems simplistic, learn to "just say no with tact."

Specifically, don't accuse the other person of being unethical. Instead, describe your feelings. Even if you think what has been proposed to you is totally outrageous, state your concern without accusation or judgment. Focus on *I* rather than *you.*

- *I have serious concerns about that.*

- *I honestly believe it's wrong.*

- *I can't do what I feel is wrong.*

Then propose alternatives:

- *I think I know what you want to accomplish, and I think there's a better way to do it.*

- *Suppose we were to try this.*

- *Here's how we can accomplish the same thing in a much simpler way.*

Dealing with questions of principle is as important as any other aspect of your career. It's a skill, just like interviewing or negotiating a raise.

IMAGE IS NOT REALITY

Being an unforgettably ethical person isn't just a matter of fostering an image. Making an impression without first building a firm foundation of principle is the equivalent of using Band-Aids when you need aspirin. It's dealing with symptoms rather than creating overall good health.

The basis of acting with principle lies in how you feel about yourself. An ethical person has an internal voice that says, "I'm not the kind of person who does those kinds of things." Passionate principle is too threatening for most of us to share openly until we have a high level of comfort with our own identity. You can't expect people to accept you as an example of passionate principle until you first give that same acceptance to yourself.

Discrepancies between your words and your inner beliefs

reveal themselves in so many different ways. Unless your self-concept is solidly in place, "You can't fool all the people all the time." So why bother trying? Instead, invest in establishing a strong passionate-principle and unforgettable identity.

A sense of principle can be nurtured in a variety of ways. One tool for revitalizing your sense of ethical self-esteem is to take a look at your past accomplishments. Be specific about this. Think of three professional accomplishments and three personal accomplishments of which you are genuinely proud. In light of those accomplishments, what traits, strengths, and characteristics do you have? What kind of person do they reveal you to be? This isn't just bragging. Feeling proud now of what you've done can prevent actions that might someday make you ashamed.

Eleanor Roosevelt said, "No one can make you feel inferior without your permission." Many of us, even the most financially successful, carry around a mental suitcase full of negative messages about ourselves. They may have originated with parents, teachers, bosses, colleagues, or even our own imaginations. But we always have the capacity to reframe those messages and make positive beliefs our conscious choice.

Sometimes we get positive pictures of ourselves from others. Hold on to them! You might want to start a folder or notebook to collect acknowledgments, thank-you notes, good reviews, positive evaluations, and other tangible evidence of your abilities. As you're compiling these positive messages, also take time to identify negative beliefs that can be undermining your sense of self.

Here's a suggestion. Write down four self-criticisms or negative beliefs that may be affecting you. Then adjust those negatives to reflect a more positive, accepting view of yourself or the situation. Support your new, positive view with specific evidence.

For example, you may have a negative belief that you're a disorganized person. Actually, you may be very organized. You just have an awful lot to do. So you might write something like this:

"Last week, in addition to my other responsibilities, I planned a new software implementation. I ran a meeting, revised 12 documents, and made 53 calls. It takes plenty of organization to coordinate all that!"

As Debra Benton wrote in her book *Lions Don't Need to Roar*, "Life is a series of relationships, and business is a series of relationships with money attached." In business, and in life, we are constantly challenged to work with and through other people. But it can be difficult to work with others when negative opinions of yourself get in the way.

It's tempting to think that people who behave unethically are different from the rest of us. But research shows that's not actually the case. Each of us is continuously making an assessment of potential risks and rewards in all areas of our lives. When people feel they have nothing to lose, they'll sometimes cross legal and ethical lines. By the same token, people who feel they have a great deal to gain will often make the same choice.

WHAT REALLY MATTERS?

In ethical terms, the one thing you can never afford to lose is the reputation you have in the eyes of those around you—and the paradox is, that reputation derives mostly from your own view of yourself. For that reason, seeing yourself as a class act is more than a reward for what you've done. It's also a protection against what you might otherwise do. Over and above dollars and cents, ethics has a direct bearing on how you feel about yourself. You need and deserve to enjoy your success to the fullest. That can't happen if you know that you've cut corners along the way. There's an old saying that's useful in this regard: "If you don't stand for something, you will fall for anything." To be a class act, stand for yourself first of all. See yourself as a creation that you can't afford to risk. By doing that, you'll also see that passionate principle is grounded in positive self-interest. You won't be tempted into doing things for money or power, because you know that you're already rich.

THE LIMITS OF THE LAW

On a national scale, it's clear how Americans have responded to the issue of business ethics: we are writing more laws. We are enacting more criminal statutes with harsher penalties. In a speech on Wall Street, for example, President George W. Bush once proposed doubling the prison terms for mail fraud, wire fraud, and obstruction of justice.

Strengthening laws is understandable—but it is also unlikely to solve the ethical problems of corporate life. The reason is, criminal laws cause people to focus on what is legal rather than what is right. Fifty years ago, the criminal definition of fraud consisted of a handful of statutes, and it covered amazingly little ground. In a publicly held company, for instance, pursuing your own interests instead of your shareholders' was not a crime. It was of course considered to be wrong, but it was not subject to prosecution.

If a shareholder lost money due to the unethical actions of a CEO, the shareholder could certainly be angry, but the principle of "let the buyer beware" was also operative. You knew or should have known that the person you're investing in might be a crook. You took that risk and you got burned. That may not have been a good way of looking at it, but that's the way it was.

Today the picture looks a lot different. The federal criminal code includes more than three hundred fraud and misrepresentation statutes. Most go far beyond anything our law used to cover. With all this criminal law, we ought to have achieved a high level of corporate honesty by now. Current events suggest otherwise. Maybe that's because we've turned what used to be moral questions into legal technicalities. In today's world, executives are more likely to ask what they can get away with legally than to worry about what's fair and honest.

The result is that corporate wrongdoers escape punishment because they find creative ways to skirt the law. Honest executives, instead of focusing on doing their jobs honorably, wind up playing the same legal games dishonest executives play. That is the natural consequence of relying too much on criminal law and too little on civil regulation and, especially, moral norms.

Another, related problem is that white-collar criminal cases that go to trial almost always focus on behavior that is on the line between legal and illegal. Defendants usually plead guilty before trial when they have clearly violated the law, and prosecutors generally do not charge defendants they cannot convict. As more criminal laws cover technical violations, more of those white-collar criminal trials will deal with technicalities. The result may be to trivialize corporate crime and undermine respect for law in general. The word *wrong* loses its bite. Expanding the criminal-fraud laws may be an easy political sell, but it is not a solution. We may wind up with tougher penalties, but we won't get more principled behavior.

ETHICS AND THE BOTTOM LINE

If talking about principle starts to sound like sermonizing, let's make one thing clear: preaching is not the purpose of this chapter. Ethics is not just an issue of morality. It also has direct impact on profit and loss. Can anyone imagine bigger financial disasters than what happened to Enron or WorldCom? Hundreds of millions of dollars were lost—not just by the guilty parties, but also by investors and former employees.

If you feel that ethical problems only occur somewhere else, not in your company, you may be right. But you may also be mistaken.

A recent study found that 43 percent of respondents believed their supervisors don't set good examples of integrity. The same percentage felt pressured to compromise their organization's ethics on the job. In other words, four out of five people surveyed believed that their company could become another scandal. It might not make the front pages, but the tragedy would be just as real.

Practicing good business ethics creates dividends that go beyond avoiding legal disaster. Employees who perceive their companies to have a conscience possess a higher level of job satisfaction and feel more valued as workers. Studies have found that efforts to instill good business ethics are welcomed by the workforce. The best way for managers to instill those ethics is by setting a good example themselves.

Here's how this works in the real world. In 1991, a bid-rigging scandal brought Salomon Brothers, a leading securities firm, to the edge of bankruptcy. Warren Buffett, the billionaire investor, was brought in as interim CEO. As one of his first actions, Buffett wrote a letter to managers throughout the company. The letter provided his home phone number and urged anyone to call if he or she saw anything unethical taking place. People did call. Before long, a collective plan was in place for rehabilitating Salomon's reputation.

WHERE DO YOU STAND?

As we near the end of this chapter, give some thought to your own behavior. Feel free to congratulate yourself on the things you're already doing right—and renew your commitment to keep on doing them. At the same time, note things you need to work on . . . the areas where you have the greatest opportunities to make ethical improvements. Once you've identified them, start fixing them, and start keeping track of your progress. A good way to start is by setting up a "What by When" section in your planner or personal organizer, or in a small notebook. Record every commitment you make: that is, what you said you'd do, and when you said you'd do it. Check the list daily as a reminder.

Here's another thought. Unless it involves strategic, company-confidential information, do your work in a way that nothing is hidden from those around you. If you're comfortable "going public" with your actions and decisions, the chances are you're operating in an ethical manner. This will also set an example for your coworkers. Secrecy is contagious, but so is transparency.

When determining how you will approach tasks or what decisions you will make, ask yourself, "How can I do this in a way that is in line or compatible with the organizational mission, values, and business principles?" Make that caveat a regular part of your action-planning vocabulary.

Lastly, watch out for four common stumbling blocks to passionate principle:

- *First, greed—the drive to acquire power, prestige, or material gain for yourself alone.*
- *Second, speed—the impulse to cut corners in response to the pace of contemporary business.*
- *Third, laziness—taking the path of least effort and resistance.*
- *Fourth and most dangerous, haziness—acting or* reacting *without thinking.*

These are the primary factors leading to unethical behavior. They're all temptations that must be recognized and overcome.

Finally, when it comes to business ethics, what activities, functions, decisions, and behaviors are really important? The answer is, all of them are important! When is it okay to be unethical? The answer is, it's never okay! What are the elements of your job to which fairness, honesty, respect, and "doing right" don't apply? There are no such elements!

Will you be able to live up to that standard? It takes real class. It demands a sense of passionate principle. But if you can do it, you will make yourself unforgettable to everyone you encounter—which is exactly what this book is all about.

CHAPTER SEVEN

Class and Confidence

In chapter 6 we discussed ethical behavior, and we saw that people who feel less than wonderful about themselves are much more likely to engage in less than wonderful acts. Moreover, they're definitely likely to feel less than wonderful if they have to account for what they've done.

Now we're going to look more closely at self-esteem, and we'll see that self-esteem can actually exist in several different varieties. Surprisingly, not all of them are positive. Most important, we're going to look at *confidence* as the key expression of self-esteem in the everyday world, especially in business situations.

Why is confidence so important? Well, when you lack confidence in yourself, other people are likely to agree with you. Quite reasonably, they figure you know more about yourself than they do, so if you're down on yourself, they probably will be also. But for the same reason, when you project an air of confidence and self-assurance, they'll feel good about you. And always remember, other people *want* to feel good about you. They want to connect with you as a professional and perhaps also as a friend. Your job is just to make that as easy as possible!

We're going to be looking at confidence from three different perspectives. First, we'll identify some of the factors that lead to low self-confidence. We'll see how these factors can act as negative influences completely outside your conscious awareness, sometimes even for many years. Then we'll introduce some powerful mental and emotional tools for countering and replacing negativity. Finally, we'll offer some interpersonal techniques you can use whenever you need to feel confident and self-assured. In short, here in chapter 7 we'll be going from the principles to the practicalities. You'll be a class act when you have both of those at your disposal.

THE TRUTH ABOUT SELF-CONFIDENCE

Here at the start, let's clear up a basic misunderstanding about confidence. It's something that causes people to wrongly interpret other people's actions, and it also causes them to act inappropriately themselves. To clarify this misunderstanding, we need to make a distinction between two key terms.

The first term is the word *confidence* itself, the topic of this chapter. We'll be evolving a definition of confidence as we go along.

The second key term is *grandiosity*, which time and again is mistaken for real confidence in today's world. Just learning the difference between confidence and grandiosity is a huge leap forward in making yourself a truly unforgettable person. So please pay close attention to the following:

Sean and Michael worked together as bond traders for a major investment bank. Sometimes there was a lot of pressure. Although they had worked side by side for several years, Sean and Michael had never really talked—until one day it came out that they were both planning to run in a marathon that was going to take place a few months later. Neither of them had ever run a marathon before, so perhaps they could train together. However, Sean did not think he needed to train for the marathon, while Michael knew he needed to. They planned to run together when the marathon actually took place.

When the day of the marathon came, as they had decided, they met in the crowd of runners a few minutes before the race was to start.

Michael confessed to feeling nervous. He knew that he had trained hard, but now the idea of actually running twenty-six miles seemed pretty outlandish. He told Sean that his goal was just to do his best and to finish the race. If he didn't make it this time, there would always be another chance. No one could predict what would happen. As he told Sean, "I guess I'll find out soon enough."

Sean had a very different attitude about the race. He was only allowing himself totally positive thoughts. He was not only picturing himself crossing the finish line in front of thousands of other runners, he was convinced that he would finish first. Sean's idea was, you can do whatever you think you can do. Many great athletes had proven that to be true.

When the race started, both Sean and Michael decided to go really slow at first. After a few miles, though, Sean confessed to feeling bored. He felt a little silly trotting alongside grandmothers and overweight people who had no real chance of finishing.

Sean apologized to Michael, then took off much faster.

As Michael had expected, running a marathon turned out to be really tough. After about fifteen miles, some of his worst fears started to come true. What had he been thinking? He should have trained much harder. Before long Michael was hardly running at all, just slowly jogging, and for a few minutes he even walked. But he did finish the marathon.

Michael was not surprised that he didn't see Sean anywhere along the course. He figured Sean had reached the finish line much sooner. But something quite different had happened. Sean had dropped out before he got close to the end. A number of unfortunate things had happened. First, he ran out of gas from going too fast. Then, when he was forced to slow down, he was getting passed by those same grandmothers who had been so annoying earlier. He was even passed by people who had slowed down to nearly a walk. This was quite a hit to Sean's ego, and one that he had not anticipated.

Sean has no plans to run another marathon. Michael is looking forward to a better performance next time.

In these two runners, the difference between grandiosity and confidence is clear. Confidence doesn't mean certainty that you're going to succeed. It means certainty that you'll do your best. Confidence is also the ability to recognize your limitations without becoming preoccupied by them. Grandiosity, on the other hand, is an unrealistic inflation of who you are and what you can do. Grandiose people ignore the possibility of anything but success. When setbacks occur, these people are taken by surprise and have a hard time recovering.

SELF-ESTEEM AND THE ENTREPRENEUR

There's something inherently heroic about being in business for yourself. It's the romance of risk taking and the refusal to compromise your dreams for the sake of security. There are also some less purely philosophical rewards for entrepreneurship. As your own boss, for example, you can set your own hours. You can take a day off or even a vacation whenever you want. And whatever profits the business makes belong to you alone.

That's the upside. The not-so-upside is the huge amount of work it takes to achieve success. Research shows that most entrepreneurs put in far more than the standard forty-hour week. Just as you get the credit (and the profits) for everything that goes right, you also get the blame (and the loss) for whatever goes wrong. So entrepreneurship is definitely not for sissies. The vast majority of entrepreneurs fail before they succeed. There will be lots of false starts before you cross the finish line.

Class, among other things, is reserve energy. It's the ability to keep trying even when you've tried and failed. It's also the power to see when the time has come to let go and try something else. Both those qualities are rare, but the second may be even more unusual than the first.

Not everyone is cut out to play in the National Basketball Association. Many people sing in the shower, or even in self-produced YouTube videos, but only a few will sing for the Metropolitan Opera. Thinking about this, you will enter a murky area in which inner and outer reality butt up against each other. Yes, it takes guts to keep shooting free throws in the backyard in hopes of playing professional basketball. But it also takes guts to exchange an impractical dream for a more feasible one. "Retreat in another direction" is by no means the same as surrender. Most important, class means learning from your mistakes. It may or may not mean giving up on a certain undertaking, but it means never giving up on yourself.

NO BLAME

You can't achieve an objective that you've never imagined. But let's repeat: you should also accept that not *every single dream* can be achieved. However, when you do make a promise from the heart, especially to yourself, many, many worthy goals are achievable regardless of the evidence of the moment.

It may not happen immediately. It probably won't. You'll make mistakes in your business, in your relationships, and in all other areas of your life. Setbacks are going to happen. Some of them will be your responsibility. Other times someone else may be at fault. But blame and victimhood are two concepts to avoid, mainly because they waste so much time and energy. The optimal viewpoint is this: "If it will take a hundred mistakes to get where I want to go, let's get started making those mistakes. Let's make them as quickly as possible and recognize them for what they are: essential steps on the path to success."

Confidence is knowing that you will succeed. If it doesn't happen today, it will happen tomorrow. If it does not come with this project, it will come with the next one. Confidence is knowing that you can acquire whatever skills and knowledge you do not yet possess. It is knowing that you are capable of working hard and tenaciously enough to go the distance, however far that may be. It is knowing that as much as you appreciate the cheerleaders in your life, you would keep going even if nobody believed in you. And sometimes nobody will believe in you. That's when confidence turns into real class.

TRULY POSITIVE THINKING

As we continue our discussion of confidence, remember that a confident person is very different from a grandiose one. Don't mistake "the power of positive thinking" for the error of not thinking at all. Regarding this, it's ironic that overly confident people and people with low confidence share the same thinking pattern. Both are absolutely sure of themselves, but in opposite directions. Some people are sure they can do anything, others are sure they can do nothing. Real confidence is not about knowing the future. It's not a rigid mind-set that refuses any possibility except complete success or total failure. Really confident people are open to the unexpected possibilities that are sure to happen.

People with low confidence can actually be upset by good news about themselves. When something indicates that they may not be as inadequate as they thought, it can seriously destabilize their internal self-image. Groucho Marx said, "I don't care to belong to any club that will accept me as a member." That's a perfect expression of the self-sabotaging view that some people cling to. This can become such an ingrained view of the world that it's no longer even a conscious choice. It can turn into a reflex, something that happens automatically.

Rejection and criticism can sometimes be easier to take than positive feedback. Low self-confidence includes a specific negative attitude about success. Whenever you succeed at something, you write it off as good luck, chance, or even a mistake of some kind. If you find it difficult to accept well-deserved compliments or honest appreciation, there's a good chance this is a comfort zone you need to get out of.

With regard to accepting compliments and praise, remember this phrase from the British writer Samuel Johnson: "What is graciously given should be graciously received." Feeling confident that you've done well doesn't mean that you're an egomaniac. On the contrary, the ability to accept credit where credit is due is a basic element of genuine class.

REINFORCING CONFIDENCE

We've seen that both an overly confident person and a person with low confidence have surprising similarities. Both have unconscious belief systems that need to be questioned and reevaluated. Now let's look at some physical and mental tools you can use to reinforce confidence whenever the need arises.

For example, suppose you need to start using a new spreadsheet computer book that you're totally unfamiliar with. This seems like a totally alien and intimidating task. So before you get started with the new book, do this. Think back to when you did something else new for the first time. Preferably, this should be something that seemed at least as intimidating as what you're now facing.

What about the first time you rode a bicycle? The whole idea of it seemed to contradict the laws of gravity. How would you ever be able to balance on those two thin wheels? Maybe you did fall over a few times, but once you learned how to do it, riding a bicycle seemed perfectly natural. It seemed to happen by itself, without your even thinking about it.

Driving a car is another good example. This is actually an amazingly complex set of behaviors. Some genuine danger is involved, and the skills of safe driving can take time to develop.

Besides using your hands and your feet, you need to keep checking the rearview mirror every few seconds. You have to know who's in front of you and behind you, and you also have to be aware of the blind spots, which can be especially dangerous. But most people learn how to do this. If you drive a car today, the chances are you're neither frightened out of your wits or totally oblivious of the risks. Driving is something you've learned how to do—both the physical actions and the mental requirements. Yet at one time driving must have seemed hugely intimidating, just as the software book does now.

Certain situations can bring anxiety and stress. This is perfectly normal. It's about what you're doing, not what you are at the deepest level of your being. Think about all the things you've accomplished over the years. You're learning now just as you learned then. You learned to do those things, and you will learn this. You can be completely confident about that.

Here's another good way to deal with intimidating situations. Attack just one part of it and achieve success. Instead of trying to deal with the whole issue immediately, warm up by doing something less intimidating that will allow you to achieve success. It can be a task that you've been putting off, such as making a call, or making a decision and taking action. Taking small steps, getting "on a roll," and getting some successes under your belt will put you into a "flow" state where you forget about everything else. Afterward, you'll feel more competent, more capable, and definitely more confident.

Once again, remember the key point about confidence. It's not a matter of feeling no doubts about yourself. It's not being totally free of hesitation. That kind of attitude is characteristic of grandiose thinking on one end of the spectrum, and low-self esteem on the other. People on both extremes are convinced that they're either totally great or completely incompetent. If you're buying into that all-or-nothing thinking, remember that you could be wrong!

MAGICAL THINKING: "I PUT A SPELL ON ME"

Thinking in new ways about yourself is a powerful tool for building self-confidence. The same tool can be applied to your thinking about other people. When you look around, you may see nothing but superconfident, totally fearless people. But you can be certain that those same people have had plenty of uncertain moments. You just don't see them right now. By the same token, don't assume that everyone else can see your own stresses and anxieties. That's what psychologists call magical thinking.

Magical thinking has nothing to do with reality, and it's a major barrier to becoming the kind of unforgettable person you want to be. So don't let yourself make magical statements about yourself or other people. If you feel this starting to happen, say to yourself calmly and gently, "Hold on a minute, that's not true." If you can come up with some evidence that disproves the magical statement, then even better. It may take a bit of effort at first, but the impact on your self-confidence levels will be huge.

Confidence isn't just about thinking well of yourself. It's also about *not* thinking badly. Stop thinking "Why did that happen?" or "Why do I feel this way?" and start thinking "How would I like to feel?" or "When do I feel confident?" or "What can I do now to feel more confident in this situation?"

Stick with it and don't expect everything at once. Building self-confidence is a process—and if it seems like a long process from where you are now, that just proves how important it is to get under way. In a moment we'll look at some practical steps you can start taking right away.

FIVE KEY SOCIAL SKILLS

In business or social situations, why is it that some people make such a positive impression? What behaviors actually imprint people on your memory to the point where they're unforgettable, while some other people you can't forget soon enough? What are the actual behaviors that define someone as a confident class act? The answers are found in a few key social skills.

These are among the most important abilities a person can have. Human beings are social animals, and a lack of social skills can lead to a lonely life. Mastery of social skills can be of great help in every area of your life and career. While these abilities are inborn in some people, they can also be learned—as you're about to find out.

The first skill is not really anything you do, but how you feel. It's the capacity to relax in a social or business setting. Stress and anxiety are contagious. When you seem ill at ease, that feeling is transmitted to others around you. If you seem confident and composed, there's a good chance you'll encounter that same state of mind in everyone else.

In developing the ability to relax, the first step is to identify exactly what makes you anxious. This varies from person to person, but among people who really have a problem with interpersonal situations, one anxiety stands out above all others. It's anxiety about anxiety. It's nervousness about being nervous. It's the fear of being found out as an anxious person, which elevates the very behaviors you're trying to hide.

If this self-confirming anxiety is a problem for you, here's a suggestion: honesty is the best policy. Without overly dramatizing your feelings, just mention that you're sometimes a bit uneasy meeting new people or speaking in public. Think about how you'll do this beforehand. Injecting a little humor is always a good idea. The main point is to be out front about the issue, and thereby to defuse it. Rest assured that nobody is going to hold this against you. In fact, admitting these very human feelings is a great way to get people on your side.

Keep in mind also that certain actions act as triggers for anxiety, even though you may think they're calming you down. Try not to do anything too quickly, whether it's walking, talking, eating, or even sitting down in a chair. Rapid, jerky motions awaken a primitive fight-or-flight syndrome. That's the last thing you want, so take your time. Subvocally, tell yourself to relax. You'll be surprised at the heightened level of confidence you feel, and the positive effect it has on others around you.

So the ability to relax is the first social skill of a confident person, and the second skill is closely related to it. It's the ability to listen. People who are ill at ease often have a habit of talking too much, too fast, or too loud. It's a misdirected attempt to take control of the situation because they're afraid of what might happen if they don't. The sad part is, it's extremely frustrating to be around a person when you can't get a word in edgewise.

Conversation is really like automobile traffic. Sometimes your light is green, sometimes it's red. Cooperation gives all the chance to get where they're going at a balanced pace. Many people would, of course, like to just talk all the time, just as some people ignore stop signs and speed limits. But that impulse can deprive you of your driver's license, just as it can deprive you of anybody to talk to.

As you're reading, tap into the third skill of confident interaction. This is empathy and genuine interest in the experiences of another person—and it's about as rare as a three-dollar bill. Training yourself to really feel what someone is trying to communicate is probably the quickest way to make yourself truly unforgettable—maybe just because it's so rare.

We spoke about empathy in our discussion of listening. Empathy is a feeling. Rapport, our fourth social skill, is the outward expression of that feeling. When you feel empathy, you are more apt to build rapport. Rapport is an understanding or connection that happens in a social interaction. It says basically, "I am like you, we understand each other." Rapport occurs unconsciously and when it happens, the language, speech patterns, body movement and posture, and other aspects of communication can synchronize down to incredibly fine levels.

Rapport is unconscious but can be encouraged by conscious efforts. One way is by mirroring or matching the verbal behavior of the other person. It's nothing complicated—just reflecting back language and speech mannerisms, including rate, volume, tone, and choice of words. Sometimes, when two people feel good about each other, this happens all by itself. Rapport has spontaneously taken place. Other times the mirroring technique is a good way to create rapport where it would otherwise be absent.

An important subcategory of building rapport is appropriate eye contact. This doesn't mean you have to stare at people—in fact, prolonged staring at someone can seem to communicate anger. But keeping your eyes on them while talking or listening is a matter of basic respect.

If you don't maintain eye contact, several ideas can pass through people's minds, and none of them are positive. They may think you're ignoring them, or that you're trying to get away from them. If they have any worries about their own confidence, this is sure to bring them on in a painful way. People like this will blame themselves for the lack of rapport. But if you've failed to even look them in the eye, it's really you who should be taking responsibility.

Other people will have a different interpretation. Instead of blaming themselves, they'll conclude that you're shifty and untrustworthy. Although in some places in the world it's considered rude to look people directly in the eye, the United States isn't one of those places. So act accordingly, and you'll be considered not cunning, but confident and classy.

SELF-AWARENESS AND SELF-ESTEEM

Low self-esteem can impact your relationships, your job, your health, and every other aspect of your life. It will be impossible for people to think of you in anything like a positive way if you don't think well of yourself.

The good news is, you can always raise your self-esteem to a healthy level, even if you're an adult who's been harboring a negative self-image since childhood. Changing the way you think—reimagining yourself and your life—is essential to boosting self-esteem. The three steps below can help you through that process:

Identify troubling conditions or situations. Think about the conditions or situations that you find troubling and that seem to deflate your self-esteem, such as dreading a business presentation, frequently becoming angry, or always expecting the worst. You may be struggling with a change in life circumstances—such as the death of a loved one, job loss, or children leaving home—or a relationship with another person, such as a spouse, family member, or coworker.

Become aware of beliefs and thoughts. Once you've identified troubling conditions or situations, pay attention to your thoughts related to them. This includes your self-talk—what you tell yourself—and your interpretation of what the situation means. Your thoughts and beliefs may be positive, negative, or neutral. They may be rational—based on reason or facts—or irrational—based on false ideas.

Identify negative or inaccurate thinking. Notice when your thoughts turn toward the negative. Your beliefs and thoughts about a situation affect your reaction to it. Negative thoughts and beliefs about something or someone can trigger the following:

- *Physical responses—such as muscle tension, a sore back, racing heart, stomach problems, sweating, or changes in sleeping patterns.*

- *Emotional responses—including difficulty concentrating or feeling depressed, angry, sad, nervous, guilty, or worried.*

- *Behavioral responses—which may include eating when not hungry, avoiding tasks, working more than usual, spending increased time alone, obsessing about a situation, or blaming others for your problems.*

WHAT PEOPLE NEED—AND WHAT YOU CAN GIVE

Since this chapter is about self-confidence and self-esteem, it may be surprising that we're going to look at the needs and feelings of other people—but to a confident person, those needs are what's really important.

People need to *receive.* People need a sense of meaning, purpose, and goals. If you're a manager in a corporate setting or a business owner, satisfying this need is a basic element of confident leadership. Whatever they may tell you or whatever they may think, no one works just for money—at least not for long.

People also need status. As a confident person and as a class act, you are in a unique position to confer feelings of sincere recognition and importance. This can take many forms. Sometimes it means singling someone out for praise in front of a group. Other times it's taking someone aside to offer thanks for a job well done.

Summing up, confidence is not really something you have. It's something you give, and then it's given back to you. Confidence, like class, is a power you radiate, and in its reflection you shine so much brighter.

CHAPTER EIGHT

Empathy for (Almost) Everyone

In chapter 5 we discussed empathy as a component of effective listening. While listening is certainly an important skill, the concept of empathy has a much wider application.

Simply put, empathy is the ability to feel in yourself what another person is feeling. If you intend to be seen as a class act, if you want to make yourself an unforgettable person, then *nothing* is more important than developing your capacity for empathy. In this chapter we'll see why that is true, and we'll also look at practical steps you can take toward becoming a more empathic human being. Along the way, we'll also look at what it means to lack empathy for other people, and why this can be so self-destructive in every area of life.

"I'M NOT PERFECT (I HOPE!)"

During the Second World War, Dwight Eisenhower was the supreme commander of Allied forces in Europe. In 1944, just before the Normandy invasion, a number of names were given to Eisenhower for possible promotion to the rank of general. One of these men requested a meeting with Eisenhower to speak in his own behalf.

He said something like this: "Sir, I have every possible qualification to be a commander. I have absolutely no fear. I've distinguished myself in combat for more than twenty years. I have tireless energy. I hardly ever need to sleep or eat. I can drive a tank, I can fly a plane, I can climb mountains, I can swim rivers, and I can walk across deserts. What more could you want?"

Eisenhower listened closely, then said, "I'm sorry, but you can never be a general. You certainly sound like an amazing soldier, but that's just the point. Most of our soldiers are not amazing, and we need generals who can understand and empathize with those men. I have to deny the promotion."

This story makes an important point. Being a leader . . . being a class act . . . being an unforgettable person . . . that requires more than just your own strengths. It also means connecting with the weaknesses or shortcomings of others. In an ultracompetitive world, it's easy to forget that. You work hard trying to develop your own capabilities, which is good. But in doing so you can lose touch with the challenges faced by the people around you.

Sometimes those challenges are clear. One of your team members may have an illness or an injury. Another may be going through a painful divorce. You'll need to be tactful in discussing those concerns, but at least the issues are out on the table. But that's usually not the case. You also need to recognize and empathize with problems that are much more subtle. Fortunately, most people's problems fall into a relatively small number of categories. The details may vary greatly from one person to another, but the emotions they experience manifest in a number of different ways. By learning to empathize with just these difficulties, you'll be able to make yourself unforgettable to the vast majority of people.

So let's look at a few of these problems.

ANXIETY

Number one, and by far the most prevalent, we can call anxiety. That's such a vague term that you might think it's meaningless, so we're going to define it a bit more precisely. Anxiety is a feeling that events are outside your control, or even outside your understanding. It's a sense of not knowing what's going to happen. You can't really make a plan for dealing with the problem because you can't picture the problem clearly. Anxiety is like fear of the dark. You're not really worried about the darkness itself. You're worried what the darkness might conceal—and not knowing what that might be makes the situation worse.

Consider this example:

Rachel is a new administrative assistant in your department. Laurie, a more experienced person, is assigned to explain Rachel's responsibilities. Laurie explains the eight tasks that Rachel needs to perform each morning within an hour of her arrival at work. Laurie, who has worked at the company for several years, knows these tasks like the back of her hand. She does them automatically, like brushing her teeth in the morning or turning off the light when she goes to sleep. But to Rachel, this is all new. She listens closely to Laurie and tries to take notes, but it's almost as if she's hearing a foreign language. All she knows for sure is that she's not absorbing what she's hearing.

What she feels is *anxiety*. She has an image of herself making a mess of everything, but the image is blurred because she's not even sure what "everything" is. She feels overwhelmed on her first day at the company, like a circuit breaker trying to process too much electricity.

As a manager, you need to show empathy here in two different directions. You obviously need to put yourself in Rachel's place, but first you need to empathize with Laurie. You need to see that Laurie may tend to expect too much of Rachel. Without knowing it, Laurie may be expecting Rachel to understand a whole new language before she's even learned the alphabet. It's also possible that Laurie may sense a little opportunity to show off here. For the moment at least, she's in a position of power, and Rachel is totally dependent on her.

Think about this for a moment. Try to see the situation from these very different points of view, which is what empathy means. Once you've done that, ask yourself how you would respond in order to serve the needs of both Rachel and Laurie, as well as your company as a whole.

A possible solution might be something like this: Instead of telling Rachel all at once about everything she's supposed to do, maybe the instructions can be spread out over several days. Rachel could learn two tasks on Monday, then two more on Tuesday. By the end of her first week, she's learned all of her eight morning tasks with one day still left over. This plan would also rein in any tendency on Laurie's part to go too fast. By empathizing with both parties, you can come up with a solution that satisfies everyone's interests.

OPTIMISM

If anxiety is the vague sense that something bad will happen, we'll refer to the flip side of anxiety as *optimism.* This, of course, is an extremely positive feeling. Just as anxiety is something you want to diminish, optimism is something you want to encourage.

Rick was a high school football coach who had been an outstanding quarterback during his college career. Whenever Rick's high school team practiced pass defense, Rick always played the role of the opposing quarterback. One day a former college teammate of Rick's came to watch a practice, and he noticed that a lot of Rick's throws were being intercepted by the high school players. Later, he kidded Rick a little about the deterioration of his arm. "I guess we're all getting old," the teammate said, "but it's a good thing you're coaching now instead of playing." Rick just laughed. "I can throw as well as I ever could," he said, "but I want to make it easy for these kids. I want them to think they can intercept every ball. Even high school quarterbacks can pass better than I was doing out there, but in practice I want them to feel pumped up, not beaten down. Now they think they've been intercepting passes off a former college star. They feel ten feet tall, which is just the way I want them to feel. I'm giving them a self-image they'll want to live up to."

Anxiety and optimism are two sides of the same coin. The empathic solution to both lies in making things easier, not harder. The way to eat a whole chocolate cake is in slices—and that's true whether you like chocolate or not. As a class act, keep that in mind whenever you want to help people maximize their potential.

FEAR

This is a variation of anxiety that's both easier and more difficult to handle. It's easier than anxiety because the scenario is more obvious. Anxious people don't know exactly what they're worried about. Fearful people know all too well. The difficulty with fear is that you may both be able to empathize with it.

There's an old joke about a man who was continuously snapping his fingers. One day his friend asked him why he was always doing that. "Well," said the man with a note of fear creeping into his voice, "I do it to keep the elephants away." His friend looked at him in disbelief: "But there are no elephants within a thousand miles of here." "Yeah," said the man, nervously snapping his fingers again. "It works great, doesn't it?"

A man who's afraid of elephants seems silly—except to another man who's afraid of elephants. To empathize with someone's fear, don't try to be afraid of the exact same thing. That almost never works because fear is a very personal thing. Instead, think about something you're afraid of—or rather, think about something that frightened you in the past. Maybe you were afraid of jumping into a swimming pool. Maybe it was getting on an airplane. Maybe you woke up one night and in the darkness you saw a monster on the other side of the room—which was really your coat over the back of a chair. This is a key point about fear. It's almost always timebound. Fears that seem convincing at certain points in our lives look much less threatening later. In fact, they usually look quite comical. But at the time they're genuinely scary.

Use this exercise on yourself first. Then you can use it to help others with their fears. Again, don't try to convince people that they're wrong to be afraid. That won't work. Instead of talking about what they fear *now*, ask them about what they *used to fear*. Show them how fears lose their power once we get more information and perspective. Then ask them to project themselves forward in time—and promise them that someday what's frightening them now will seem as harmless as their fears in the past. This is an empathic way of helping people with their fears. Try it, and you'll see how much better it works than lecturing people or ignoring them.

ANGER

Of all the negative feelings people can experience, *anger* is probably the most common in the modern world. We live in the midst of an anger epidemic. People may look placid as grazing cattle, but they are seething with rage all around us. You're put on hold during a telephone call, you're waiting in the checkout line, you're caught in traffic behind a guy going twenty miles an hour—in every case, the result is anger. And those are just the minor situations. I'm sure you can think of many, many others in which the gloves really come off.

Let's take an empathic look at anger. Research on anger has

shown that certain situations really tick people off. One of the most potent is feeling *wrongly accused.* You work harder than anyone else on a project and it falls through. If you get blamed, how do you feel? You get a parking ticket with time still on the meter. How do you feel? There are lots of other examples of wrongful accusations. Can you think of any now? If you can, the chances are you feel angry just recalling them. That's good. That's empathy in action.

As with fear, it's important to be empathic about anger because there's such a big difference between being inside it and outside it. From the inside, anger is like fire. It can start out like the tiny flame of a match, but with that tiny flame you can burn the whole house down. Once again, think about how you feel when you're really angry. If you're like many people, you'll sacrifice everything for the sake of that compelling feeling. You'll throw the expensive plates against the wall. You'll kick the dog. You'll slam the door—and if you slam it on your finger, that will make you even more angry.

As a class-act manager, you'll often be called upon to deal with angry people. Remember the metaphor of the match flame that I mentioned a moment ago. Don't let yourself catch fire. Don't let another person burn you down. It's important to emphatize, but empathy is not the same thing as direct participation.

Refusing to enter the world of angry people is probably the best thing you can do to help them. It's not easy for one person to stay angry for long in the presence of someone who refuses to participate. It's much easier to keep the anger going when you're by yourself. That's why angry people tend to storm out of the room if they can't get you going. Try to prevent that from happening if you can. Then, gently say the following two sentences: "I understand that you're upset. We'll talk when you're feeling better."

Don't say anything else. If the angry person tries to force you to talk, repeat those two sentences. Without taking time to explain why, these are the optimal words to use when confronting anger. They're nonjudgmental, and they also hold open the possibility of further dialogue—but only when the anger subsides. Once again, whatever you do, don't go down to the level of anger that you're seeing. Because you've got too much class for that.

DEPRESSION: "WHAT'S THE USE?"

So far we've looked at four topics as opportunities for empathy: anxiety, optimism, fear, and anger. Surprisingly, the two that have the greatest affinity are anger and optimism. Anger is actually a hopeful emotion. It's based on the belief that you can have an influence if you just get angry enough. People rarely get angry at avalanches or earthquakes. What's the point? But maybe, just maybe, if you get angry enough at your boss or your spouse, you'll be able to alter his or her behavior. Or at least you'll be able to get his or her attention. It's impossible to get the attention of a hurricane, so people don't waste their time trying. Anger may seem irrational, but there's usually some optimism or hope behind it.

The feeling of *depression* is in stark contrast to this. Depressed people have given up hope. Their basic view of the world can be summed up in three words: "What's the use?" Depression is often mistaken for unhappiness, but that's really a misunderstanding. It's possible to be unhappy without being depressed. Depression is much closer to a physical feeling such as fatigue than it is to anger or anxiety. Similarly, the opposite of depression is not happiness or joy—it's vitality, the willingness to get up and do something. Really depressed people literally cannot convince themselves to get out of bed in the morning. Again, "what's the use?"

Empathizing with depression is not really a matter of putting yourself into a certain frame of mind. It's putting yourself into a physical state rather than an emotional one. It's draining yourself of energy. It's just lying there.

With this in mind, what do you think is the most effective course to take with people who are experiencing depression? It's not a matter of talking to them. Either they won't say anything, or they'll just talk about how depressed they are and how useless everything is. No, depression is really a physical experience, so the antidote is physical action. Try to get people moving again, and the more movement the better. They'll resist, of course, because secretly they know that what you're suggesting will work. For depressed people, depression is the comfort zone, and they're reluctant to leave it. But they'll have to leave it if you can just get them ambulatory.

Unless you're clinically ill, it's impossible to be depressed going down a waterslide. It's impossible to be depressed dancing the polka. Don't try to talk people into being less depressed so that they'll start to dance. Get them dancing and they'll be less depressed. Get them dancing, and you'll be unforgettable.

The last and most difficult opportunity for empathy is with a person who's in denial. To understand this, let's call upon a maxim that has been invoked in a great many personal-development books—but it's valuable nonetheless: "If you keep doing what you've been doing, you'll keep getting what you've been getting."

The reason this maxim is valuable is not because it's true. It's because it sounds true, but isn't. A hundred million years ago, for instance, the dinosaurs kept doing what they'd been doing, but they didn't get what they'd been getting. What they got was extinction. That's what happens when conditions change but you don't. It's not easy to empathize with a denying person because they refuse to see that conditions have changed.

Virtually every organization has people of this kind. Often they've been with the company for a long time. Sometimes they have their own little mini-kingdom, which for some reason is often in the accounting department. From their vantage point, it's still 1990, or 1980, or maybe even 1975. As with a depressed person, talking them out of this can be difficult. Once again, what's called for is physical action. Give these people a new assignment. Give them something way outside their well-defended fiefdom, so that they can't possibly deny things have changed.

And be aware of this: it might not work. You might run into people who say they just won't do it. What they mean is, they just *can't* do it—and they might be correct about that. They can't do it any more than those dinosaurs could adapt to a suddenly different climate. So you might have to say good-bye to some people who are in that deep denial. You should say good-bye without guilt because you've done what you could. They are choosing to leave rather than choosing to change.

There is a difference between feeling empathy for people and agreeing with them. As a class act, you should have the ability to see the reality of the other person's feelings. No judgment should be attached to that reality. Needless to say, you can and should attach judgment to the content of those feelings. If, for example, people harbor racial or sexist prejudices, it's not just a matter of "they have a right to their opinion." The first step, however, is to see what their opinion is, and to see it from their point of view, even if you find that point of view distasteful.

Empathy is an important human relations tool, and it's definitely part of an unforgettable person's repertoire. But you also have a right to expect a certain amount of empathy yourself. Beyond a certain point, you're not required to tolerate people who are intolerant. If you were to do that, you yourself would be exercising a form of denial. But your goal is not to be a saint. Your goal is to be an unforgettable class act.

CHAPTER NINE

Building Confidence in Your Team

Earlier we discussed how confidence is a key foundation of class. We looked at ways you can assess and build a sense of confidence and self-esteem into your career and your personal life. But when it comes to making yourself unforgettable, developing the qualities in yourself is only the start. A person with genuine class also knows how to inspire others to better themselves. That's team building in the broadest and best sense of the word.

The exact definition of team building is a complex philosophical problem. On the everyday level, however, it's much simpler. Anyone can be an effective team builder and team leader. That's good news, because it's your task to bring out the full potential in the people around you. They need to find the right balance between social, moral, and business aspects of team building, and you can help them achieve that balance.

The first step—and surely the most important is to set a good example. Effective leaders "walk their talk," and this naturally invites others to come along. Then, when leaders with class see positive changes in their team, they never fail to reward or compliment everyone who is doing well. On the flip side, in terms of constructive criticism, unforgettable team builders are the first to admit when they are wrong. We've already discussed the concept of mistakes as learning experiences that foster progress. When you act in accordance with that principle, people will feel comfortable asking for your help and advice in difficult situations.

WHAT IT TAKES

Interpersonal skills are the most important elements of team building, partly because so many people have a hard time dealing with those around them. Dwight Eisenhower was right when he said that team building is getting others to do what you want because they think it is what they want. With the best people skills, people will want to do their best because they are doing something for themselves. Beyond the all-important principle of setting an example, several personal qualities can help you be a positive influence in the lives of others.

Flexibility is definitely one of these traits. How well do you "go with the flow"? How capable are you of making new plans when an unforeseen problem calls for a change of direction? If you need some help with this, make an effort to concentrate on making plans for a number of possible outcomes on something you are about to try for the first time.

Decisiveness is also important in team building, and lack of it can be the downfall of many leaders and managers. There is no team building if you are not making important decisions. Unfortunately most important decisions are also the hard decisions. No one else wants to try to make them. Be willing to take bold action in whatever way you think will be best. Of course, when you do this, there's no guarantee that everyone will agree you made the right decision. But dealing with that is part of being a class act.

Other qualities of a world-class team builder include:

Punctuality: Develop a reputation for being on time and you will earn the respect of other organized professionals. Especially in meetings, when others arrive on time, they will expect you to be prompt, too. Nothing is more frustrating to a team than constantly waiting for a tardy participant.

Consideration: Always take the time to greet people with a friendly, personal greeting. You will have the time to do this properly if you arrive a little early to meetings so that you can greet others as they arrive.

Deference: In your home or office, you are responsible for making everyone comfortable and productive. On someone else's territory, you should step back and allow them to set the tone.

Appearance: Whether a specific setting calls for formal business attire or casual dress, you should do your best to fit in. If professional attire is expected, you should wear it; if you are coming in from a job site, take a few moments to dust off and look presentable.

Attention: You should listen at least twice as much as you talk. Ask three questions in a conversation before you volunteer information about yourself.

Etiquette: At the beginning of a meeting or social gathering, be sure that everyone has been properly introduced. At the end, don't rush out in a hurry as if you can't wait to get away as fast as possible—even if you really can't wait!

EFFECTIVE TRAINING

As a team builder, your commitment should express itself not only in how you lead every day, but also in formal training books that give team members the confidence and skill they need to become unforgettable leaders themselves.

The higher you are on the corporate masthead, the more

involved you should be in developing training books. If you're the CEO of your company, for example, your presence will guarantee that training will be taken seriously by people who want to move up in the company.

As you begin to develop training and team-building books, it's important to focus on values as well as on techniques. For instance, the first value you need to identify might be "What defines team-building competency?"

Be sure that your training book is in alignment with your company's mission statement and business strategy. Make sure you're developing a plan that is more than just a teacher-student scenario. Training of this kind shouldn't happen only once a year at the company's weekend retreat. It should be part of everyday corporate life. Team members should be assigned developmental tasks, external education, and, up the ladder, should also have meetings with international counterparts and full assessments of abilities. This makes both your book and your management stronger.

MAKING NEW MEMBERS PART OF THE TEAM

Team members are the backbone of any successful enterprise. While the designated leaders might make all the big decisions, team members are the ones that get the labor required to get the work done. Without good employees, a company could not function properly. Unfortunately many employees forget the hard work that they did once they move into corporate or management positions. This is why employee training and employee development is essential to a successful company. When the employees become more successful, the company becomes successful.

In many leading-edge companies, new hires are required to attend an employee-training seminar immediately after coming on board. Often a great deal of information needs to be passed on as soon as possible. A seminar is an opportunity to learn the details of what makes a company work. New hires also learn what may be expected of them beyond their formal job descriptions.

This orientation is beneficial, but it should be only part of a continuing development experience. Unfortunately, many companies simply stop at the beginning. In creating and maintaining training-and-development books, a team builder needs to keep two things in mind. The book needs to be a unique priority, while at the same time it needs to become part of the daily workplace routine. Employee training books are important for getting new employees into the loop of how the company operates and what the company's expectations are, as well as for keeping established employees in the chain of knowledge and communication. Effective books will improve communication and understanding between individuals and departments. However, if team builders don't understand the importance of employee training books for both the company and its employees, the book will never accomplish much. Depending on the size of the company, it may be beneficial to have employee training coordinators. Their responsibilities would include scheduling and planning each of the training chapters, so that each employee receives the maximum benefit.

Employees who understand their job and what is expected of them are far more likely to enjoy their job and be more productive. With an established employee-training book, companies can expect to see increases in their sales numbers as well as overall productivity.

TEAM BUILDING AND TIME MANAGEMENT

People tend to have a contradictory approach to time management. They know it's important—that it can be the difference between a middle manager and a top executive—yet they waste time every day. As a team builder, you can help your team make the most of every minute by implementing the following time-management principles and techniques:

An hour of planning can save you ten hours of doing. Don't head into big projects without setting out goals, how you will achieve those goals, and the most important part, setting times by which they have to be accomplished. This will save you a lot of time trying to make decisions on the spot, which will make the project take a lot longer.

Improve your reading speed. The average reading speed is two hundred words per minute. Most people have to read for at least two hours a day for work. A speed-reading course can double your reading speed. That gives you another hour to do more productive things.

Devote one hour each day to personal self-improvement. If you spend one full hour a day on a skill you want to improve, that computes to seven hours a week (almost a full workday), and 365 hours a year (and more than two straight weeks without sleep). You can become proficient and even master the skill of your choice.

Practice patience. It's natural to want positive change to happen as easily and as quickly as possible. But change often takes longer than you expect. First, change has to be accomplished, then integrated, and then transformed into the foundation for the next step in your development.

Be adventurous. See change as a challenge and a transformation. Throw yourself into planning and preparation. Explore new career horizons that may appear. See this as an adventure, not an obligation.

Practice constructive discontent. Instead of clinging to the status quo, ask yourself, "How could I change for the better? How could changing myself help my team improve as well?"

Try something new each day. When people expand beyond their comfort zone, they tend to try to build a new comfort zone as quickly as possible. Challenge yourself to try at least one new way of doing things every day.

Ask for input. Ask for ideas and suggestions and for feedback on how well you are adjusting to change. Periods of change are times to build bridges, not walls. They are times to be open to input, not defensive. By modeling this in yourself, you can start moving your team in the same direction.

Use a to-do list, which will also become an "it's done" list. Such a list is an extremely important tool, so we'll be discussing it in some detail. It seems so simple that it's almost laughable, yet few people have even the basic level of organization that a to-do list provides. Most of us are working on more than one thing at a time, or (which is much worse) not working on anything at all. Make yourself accountable to one thing: the list.

One of the most insightful rules of workplace behavior states, "Work expands to fill the time available." If you have two weeks in which to complete a project, you will complete it in two weeks, but the same project could also take a month if you were given that much time. If you only put one thing on your to-do list, you are most likely to spread it throughout the day. If you add another thing to the list in the early part of the day, you will probably get them both done. If you have six or seven things on the list, you might still be able to get them all done in a day. That's a huge improvement over the one thing you were going to get done before.

Remember that time management isn't just about doing things faster, but also about doing the right things the first time. So organize your list along the following lines:

- Record all activities—Write down all your multiple demands, competing priorities, tasks, and activities for the day or the week. This will allow you to visualize what needs to get done.
- Determine primary goals—Make a list of your primary goals for the day or for the week.

- Evaluate important vs. urgent—Decide which of these activities are the most important versus the most urgent. Consider how certain items affect others and the consequences for not accomplishing certain items.

- Rank—Use a ranking system to begin planning. For example:

A tasks have high priority and must be completed immediately.

B tasks are moderately important but can be done after A tasks.

C tasks are of low-level importance and can be tackled in your spare time.

- Create a schedule—Indicate deadlines for each task and estimate the time needed to complete the task. Keep in mind any tasks that may be linked together to increase productivity.

- Revisit goals and adjust—Review your goals and the rewards of doing the task on time, and make any necessary adjustments. Get rid of items on your list that remain at the bottom and will realistically not get done.

SHARED RESPONSIBILITY

Just as a to-do list is an essential tool for individual productivity, teams within an organization or company can also have collective goals and shared time frames in which to accomplish them. As a team builder, your task is to identify goals, clarify them, and help team members to do the same.

Here are some tips:

Prioritize objectives. The first step is to brainstorm to generate a list of all you hope to accomplish. This can be done as a group with your team and those people that give you the projects. After generating this list, place all the ideas into categories—urgent, important, and unnecessary. Now you can develop a numbered list of specific goals for all that needs to get done.

Establish a production schedule with intermediate goals. Now that you have a list of what needs to be done, make an actual schedule so you can put dates to all the ideas. Urgent goals need to be dealt with soon, so setting time frames for these tasks is important. In addition, by setting intermediate steps to your larger goals, you can be certain of smooth progress or how production might need to be altered to meet deadlines. These intermediate goals also enable you to evaluate your team's performance and determine which tactics are effective in completing your goals.

Communicate the goal system and objectives to your team. Be certain that each member of your team understands the importance of the goals and the timelines for achieving them. Obtain input from the team members about how to best meet these goals. Finally, assign your team members to work on specific aspects of the larger goals, letting them know what they are personally responsible for producing.

Reward success. Setting goals is one of the easier parts of your job as a team builder. You now must keep your team and yourself motivated to achieve them in spite of constant change in the workplace. One of the strongest motivators is to give a reward each time a goal is met. It doesn't have to be anything of tangible value. The most effective recognition is often a simple congratulatory memo. Just make sure that the team member knows you value his or her effort and time.

WRITING A PROFESSIONAL DEVELOPMENT PLAN

A somewhat formal document for team members' plans, hopes, and dreams can be extremely useful. This Professional Development Plan is an excellent tool for keeping team members focused on their goals.

The first step is self-evaluation. This should focus not on goals or time frames, but rather on personal strengths. Team members should think about what they're good at! It's easier to do things you love than to try to perform well in activities you have no interest in and aren't good at. No one is expected to be good at everything, so acknowledging weaknesses is a valid thing to do. But strengths and abilities should be the primary focus.

Encourage your team members to think about something they might want to learn—a new skill, or even a whole new job. They should research what it would take to learn this. Effective professional development can only happen with continuing education. Team members should browse trade magazines, job descriptions, and career guides. If an individual is trying to move up the corporate ladder, he or she should learn what other people have done to advance.

The next step involves writing out plans and goals. Team members should create a list of goals they would like to meet in the next year, the next five years, and by the end of their careers.

This list, and the Professional Development Plan as a whole, should be kept in a safe place where it can be easily found and regularly reviewed.

Once the list of long-term goals is complete, more immediate objectives should be addressed. These are things that can be accomplished in less than one year. Team members should make sure that at least one of these objectives helps them reach one or more of the goals on their long-term list. The Professional Development Plan should be reevaluated, and possibly revised, regularly.

DEALING WITH CONFLICT

One of the most important qualities of an unforgettable person is the ability to resolve conflict. In the workplace, this ability is not just important, but absolutely essential. While conflict resolution might seem like an unpleasant prospect, it can actually be one of the most rewarding aspects of team building.

When you're called upon to deal with a person or persons as a mediator or supervisor, the following are useful guidelines to keep in mind:

Build rapport. Begin by putting the team member at ease. Try to reduce his or her anxiety. One way to do this is to begin with honest appreciation that is supported by evidence.

Relate to the circumstance. Try to focus on the situation and not the personalities. You should inform the team member of whatever you may already know about the problem and give him or her a chance to explain what happened. By your reducing defensiveness and not jumping to conclusions, the different perspectives will surface, and the root cause of the problem can be found and addressed.

Reassure the team member and restore performance. People who are having problems need to be reassured that this in itself does not mean they've done anything wrong. Team members should be reassured of their value and importance, and also of your support and encouragement.

When necessary, remove the team member from his or her role. Sometimes you will find that a team member is not a good fit, whether for a specific task or for membership in the organization as a whole. When this happens, you will need to assess what the person's real strengths, interests, and goals are. The next step may be a change in the person's assignment and responsibilities. In other cases, it may be in everyone's best interests if the person separates from the organization.

Aspiring to become an unforgettable human being is more than just an internal process. It means interacting and connecting with other people in every area of your life. It means bringing out the best in them just as you strive to bring out the best in yourself. For people with true class, the success of others is equal in importance to their own success. The purpose of this chapter has been to make that point, and to provide tools for putting it into action. The rest is up to you!

CHAPTER TEN

Stress Management

Class is a word that can apply to many different circumstances and situations. Sometimes the meaning is specific, while other times it's more vague or metaphorical. In horse racing, for instance, class often refers quite simply to the price of the horses in the race, or the purse that the winner will receive. But it can also mean the mysterious, intangible will to win that empowers a champion to meet whatever challenge presents itself. The more difficult the challenges overcome, the more they point to a classy winner. Part of making yourself unforgettable is the ability to see obstacles as opportunities. They're not just annoyances. They're a chance to prove what you're made of.

THE MOST DIFFICULT CHALLENGE

While acute crises can be difficult to manage, those situations are, by definition, limited in terms of time and place. But stress can go on for a long time, even indefinitely. Stress is dangerous partly because people can get used to it. You're probably familiar with the story about a frog getting boiled in water that only gradually and almost imperceptibly rose in temperature. That's a good story, but in real life frogs actually jump out of the water. Humans, on the other hand, will let themselves overheat to destructive levels based on long-standing stress in their working lives.

For a person with class, dealing with stress requires strength but also mature judgment. You need to call upon your inner resources, and you must also be aware of when it's time to disconnect from a situation in the most appropriate way.

Most people don't know how to do that, despite the clear presence of stress in the lives of millions of people. In 1992, a United Nations report called stress the "20th century epidemic." Four years later, a survey by the World Health Organization (WHO) used similar language, referring to stress as a "worldwide epidemic." In the years since then, life has certainly not gotten any less stressful!

Workplace stress overload results in 1 million absent American workers each day. Stress results in mistakes and accidents, declining productivity and burnout, low morale and lost employees, increases in alcoholism and drug use, as well as workplace violence and harassment.

Based on research studies and information cited by author Ravi Tangri in the book *StressCosts, Stress-Cures,* stress is responsible for the following work-related issues:

- *19 percent of absenteeism*
- *40 percent of turnover*
- *30 percent of short- and long-term disability*
- *10 percent of drug-plan costs*
- *60 percent of total workplace accidents*
- *total costs of workers' comp and lawsuits due to stress*

It has been estimated that 80 percent of health-care expenses are stress-related. Moreover, as the costs of drugs and medical treatment rise, the dollar amount of stress-related expenditures is consistently rising. With this in mind, it should be obvious that the causes of stress need to be addressed and minimized by anyone who wants the most out of life.

Fortunately, the main causes of stress—at least in the workplace—are well documented:

Overwork. Obviously, too much work causes stress. But employees also suffer when assignments are unclear or poorly supervised. An unforgettable leader and team builder needs to closely monitor the mechanics and procedures in a work environment, as well as the volume of the work itself.

Random interruptions. Phone calls, walk-in visits, and unanticipated demands from managers all contribute to increased stress. Make sure that what you expect from team members is absolutely clear. Then give them a stable environment in which to meet those expectations.

Uncertainty. In times of economic downturn, the possibility of layoffs or furloughs or other cutbacks are major sources of stress. You should keep your team informed about situations that might affect their jobs and provide reassurance if you can credibly do so.

Inadequate feedback. Team members need to know whether they are meeting expectations. Consistent, written and verbal, personalized feedback is needed from the team leader.

Lack of appreciation. Failure to show appreciation generates stress. There are many ways to demonstrate appreciation, but the most effective is just a sincere recognition of a team member's positive contribution. And it should be put in writing!

Lack of control. Stress is greatest when team members feel they had minimal input on issues that affect them.

These stress-producing categories deserve your attention. Don't let them persist—whether your role is that of a team leader and manager, or an employee and team member.

STRESS SIGNS AND SYMPTOMS . . . AND RELIEF

On the physical level, stress can be measured through hormones produced by the adrenal glands. But in everyday life, you'll need to watch for other stress signals—in yourself and in those around you:

- *sleep difficulties*
- *loss of appetite*
- *poor concentration*
- *uncharacteristic errors*
- *angry outbursts*
- *antisocial behavior*
- *emotional outbursts*
- *alcohol or drug abuse*

There are many stress-relief tools and techniques. One of the most simplest and most powerful is known by the acronym HALT. This offers a clear and effective means for recognizing stress and intervening proactively.

HALT stands for Hungry, Angry, Lonely, Tired. Each of these physical or emotional conditions can cause significant stress. Just as important, each can "creep up" outside of conscious awareness.

Hunger in this context means more than just lack of food. The word can also refer to emotional needs: hunger for security, for comfort, for understanding, or for companionship. These are all versions of hunger that you need to have nourished in your life if you intend to be an unforgettable person. They're also needs that you can help fulfill in the lives of other people.

Stress caused by anger is a bit more complex feeling, and for many people the solution is more challenging. By itself, there is nothing wrong with feeling angry, and certainly some things in the world justify that feeling. But few people know how to express anger constructively.

The first step toward changing this is to recognize the underlying cause of your anger. Behind the emotion as we experience it, anger always comes from some kind of perceived helplessness or frustration. More specifically, it's frustration that the world, or someone in it, is not following the agenda that we have set. It's as if we were saying, "Why don't you just wise up and see things my way?" But the world is not set up to see things "my way." An unforgettable person realizes that and adjusts to that reality. As that adjustment takes place, anger and frustration can be replaced by action and tangible accomplishment.

Lonely refers to self-isolation. As with hunger, the solution depends on contact with other people. But loneliness emphasizes the difficulty of making that contact—the reluctance to reach out.

The last letter of the HALT acronym stands for "tired." High-achieving men and women especially may tend to ignore fatigue. Here, fortunately, the solution is rather obvious: napping or sleeping! But if you have difficulty sleeping, the cause may be one of the other elements of the HALT acronym. So think carefully about these issues, then take action.

MORE STRESS-REDUCTION TECHNIQUES

The tools and techniques that follow won't change the underlying conditions that give rise to stress. But they will help you avoid the depression that stress can bring on. When you're depressed, you can't take action—so these tools will help you stay at a level at which positive action is possible. As always, you can use these ideas in your own life, and you can also share them with others.

Humor. Laughter literally changes the biochemistry of the brain. It also changes our perception of the world around us. If you want to change your perceptions, connect with something funny. And if that particular something isn't funny, find something else!

Exercise. Contrary to what you might think, the opposite of depression is not happiness. It's vitality. Stress, as a precursor of depression, can rob you of energy. Don't give in to that negative influence! When you're feeling stressed, it can take a real act of will to get up off the couch, but if you do manage to get yourself into motion, the benefits are powerful and immediate. As with laughter, exercise has biochemical effects that you experience as emotional change.

Drink enough water. Dehydration is the unrecognized cause of many physical and emotional problems, everything from kidney disease to dementia. Quite simply, the human body depends on water to function properly. If you deplete your inner water supply, you will experience stress and you won't function at a high level physically or mentally.

Get a good night's sleep (or a nap right now). Sleeping well at night is vital for a healthy mind and body, and napping during the day can also be beneficial. Sleep recharges and energizes, relaxes, and helps to wipe the brain clean of pressures and unpleasant feelings.

One last point to think about. If you feel really stressed today, it's probably not the first time you've felt that way. But can you recall what you felt stressed about two years ago? What about just one year ago—or even last month? If you're like most people, you haven't the slightest idea what was bothering you, except that it seemed really important at the time.

What does that tell you?

CHAPTER ELEVEN

Patience with a Purpose

In the last twenty years or so, literally thousands of books have been published on success and personal development. Almost every possible emotion and experience has been explored and analyzed. Yet one of our most common experiences in the modern world has yet to get the attention it deserves—especially since it's not only common, but also difficult.

It's the experience of *waiting*. Not a day goes by, and usually not even an hour, when we don't face the considerable challenge of waiting for something or somebody. Waiting at a traffic light. Waiting in a checkout line. Waiting for a job interview. Waiting in a doctor's office. The list could go on and on, and those are just the relatively harmless forms of waiting. I'm sure you can think of other instances that are much more challenging, and even frightening.

Yes, there's a lot of waiting in our lives, and a lot of difficulties go with it. The purpose of this chapter is to give you some tools for handling that pervasive experience with good humor, with class—and most of all with patience. Because patience is absolutely essential for dealing with waiting. You can often take actions to shorten a wait, but sometimes you can do nothing except . . . *wait*. A situation such as that can be very, very difficult unless you've developed a capacity for patience. Even if you have developed that capacity, it can also be difficult to be around someone else who lacks patience—whether it's a colleague at work, a family member, or the guy behind you who keeps honking his horn. So for the next few minutes we'll be working toward developing patience in yourself—and also toward fostering it in the people around you.

Let's begin with a definition of patience, and it refers back to the topic of waiting that I mentioned a moment ago. *Patience is the ability to wait without experiencing anger, anxiety, or frustration.*

The first thing to notice about that definition of patience is that it's entirely internal. It's subjective rather than objective. You can't put patience on a scale and weigh it, you can't add it up like a bank account, and you can't put it in your pocket and take it out when you need it. In many cases, you can't tell whether people are patient or impatient by looking. Someone sitting next to you in a waiting room may be seething with impatience, but all you see is a man leafing through a magazine. Likewise, when that man looks over at you, he may see a perfectly placid individual. Little does he know how furious you are that the dentist is running late!

Since patience is internal, I want to first give you an internal process for developing it. I want you to grasp a simple fact: when your ability to control external events is limited or nonexistent, you *must* learn to control your inner responses. You must learn to control your anger and your frustration and your anxiety. The good news is, those responses are *always* within your control, no matter what's happening in the physical world.

Here's a quote that will help to clarify this: "We could never learn to be brave and patient if there were only joy in the world." Helen Keller said that, and she could not see, could not hear, and could not speak as a result of a childhood illness. Obviously, her life was not only joy, but she chose to see the absence of joy as the means for developing other capacities. Because she faced unhappiness, she learned to be brave and patient. She's not saying that the absence of joy was a good thing, but she is saying that some good things came out of it. That was her internal process.

As you may know if you're familiar with Helen Keller's story, she did not come to this state of serenity easily. As a child, she was like a wild animal, furiously lashing out at everything around her. She learned to be patient the hard way, only after she had exhausted the other alternatives.

With that in mind, let's return to developing patience as an internal process by taking control of your subjective responses. Imagine that you're in line at your local Starbucks. It's eight forty-five in the morning and you need to be at work by nine, but you definitely need your coffee. And all you want is a coffee. You don't want a latte, you don't want a Frappuccino, you don't want a chai tea with just a little room for cream. You just want a coffee, but you do want it now.

Well, bad luck for you, because after you've waited for the line to run down until just one person is ahead of you, that person just can't seem to make up her mind. Should it be a cappuccino or a Frappuccino? Whipped cream, yes or no? Decaf or regular? There are just so many choices, and this woman seems to be exploring all of them in detail. All you want is a simple coffee. It's enough to make you scream.

Well, suppose you do scream. That may or may not help you get your coffee sooner. Probably not, but that's not the point we want to make here. What needs to be emphasized is the way you have taken the internal experience of impatience and waiting and turned it into an external experience that involves everybody around you.

For the purposes of being a class act, that's a mistake. Why is it a mistake? Because in the Starbucks you can't control the external circumstances, you can only influence them to a limited degree. So when you externalize what's going on in your head, not much good can come of it. There's a legend that a king of ancient Persia once ordered waves in the ocean to be whipped because they wouldn't obey him. That sounds foolish, but it's essentially the same thing as making a scene in Starbucks or banging on the steering wheel when you're stuck in a traffic jam.

Fortunately, there is another choice. Remember some of the things we've said so far. Remember our definition of patience: *patience is the ability to wait without experiencing anger, anxiety, or frustration.* Remember what Helen Keller said: *we could never learn to be brave and patient if there were only joy in the world.* Now use those two principles to create a kind of test for yourself. Challenge yourself to suppress your anger, anxiety, and frustration. Make a conscious effort in that direction because it certainly won't happen by itself. As Helen Keller said, use the joyless experience you're having for learning patience. Don't just endure it passively, and don't make a fool of yourself by externalizing it. Instead, turn it into an active opportunity for growth.

Thomas Edison must have been one of the most patient people who ever lived. It's interesting that, like Helen Keller, he had a physical handicap in his deafness. Maybe this taught him to accept what he couldn't change. But he had developed an almost supernatural ability for patience in his work. Edison didn't use conventional scientific methods. He progressed by simple trial and error. It's said that when he was developing filaments for the first incandescent lightbulb, he tried more than seventeen thousand materials before he found one that worked. How did he do it? Edison used a method similar to what we've just discussed. He didn't just passively absorb one failure after another, nor did he start throwing things against the wall. Instead, he turned the situation into a challenge, or even a game. If he tried using the skin of a potato in his lightbulb and it immediately burned to a crisp, he saw this as a discovery in itself. He didn't say, "I still haven't found something that will work," He said, "I've found one more thing that doesn't work." He didn't get depressed, he didn't start a fight with his wife, he didn't kick the dog. He went on to the next thing.

That's class—and for most people it doesn't come easily. It's not really natural. Suppose you want to train a laboratory rat to press a button to get a bite of food. Suppose you give the rat a full year to solidify that behavior. Every time it pushes the button, it gets food, month after month. It happens thousands of times. But then one day, instead of getting food, the rat gets a mild electric shock when it presses the button. After thousands of positive experiences pressing the button, how many times do you think the rat will need to press it before it totally gives up and is ready to starve to death? The answer is, only three times. Four at the very most. At that point, it either starts running around the cage like mad—the equivalent of having a snit in Starbucks—or it just sits there passively.

There's a big difference between you and a lab rat. Use the tools we've discussed so far and you can turn pain into patience, and patience into positive change. We'll have more to say about this in a moment.

We've created a definition of patience, and we've looked at some ways to develop patience in situations that demand it. Let's look now at some further elements of patience that can help to clarify exactly what it means.

Patience is the ability to detach from the need for immediate gratification. A baby wants it's bottle now or the baby will cry. The rat wants its food as soon as it pushes the button. The guy in the line at Starbucks wants his muffin right away. Maybe all that is perfectly natural. But a class act knows that life is more complicated than doing what comes naturally. So a class act is able to wait when waiting is necessary.

Patience means showing tolerance, compassion, and understanding toward people who are less mature, less strong, and less patient than you are. If you visit the monkey house in the zoo, a chimp may start making faces at you. Do you get angry at the chimp? Are you ready to start a fight with that monkey? I hope not. I also hope that, the next time somebody honks his horn at you at a red light, you don't immediately revert to apelike consciousness. Jesus said, "Forgive them, for they know not what they do"—and he was being crucified. You're just getting honked at.

Patience means accepting the obstacles and reversals that are inevitable in every area of life. You learned how to walk although you must have fallen down many times. You learned how to speak a language, yet the world's most powerful computer can do this at just a primitive level. Call upon your innate capacity for patience the next time you feel like giving up or flipping out. That capacity is still there, so learn to use it.

With your coworkers, and especially with family members or close friends, be patient when problems arise that may take time to resolve. It's amazing how often long-standing connections can fall apart after a single misunderstanding. When people know each other really well, do they lose the capacity to show the patience they would give to relative strangers? As a class act, don't let this self-indulgent behavior injure important relationships in your life. Many people let this happen, and they always regret it.

If you're feeling enthusiastic about something in your life, be patient with people who can't immediately share your exuberance and excitement. What's more, accept that they may even resent you for it. This isn't pretty or admirable, but it's just the nature of some people.

Above all, recognize that there is no need to rush yourself or others in any aspect of learning and growth. Be patient about learning to be patient. Show this patience with yourself, and with others around you.

This is an especially important point. Remember, Dale Carnegie's work on personal development was not just for the benefit of one person. It was also to show people how they can positively influence others. As a manager, as a class act, and as a friend, you can do specific things to help people develop patience.

Consider this example. Rick was a senior associate at a prestigious law firm. His legal skills were excellent, and he definitely seemed on track to make partner. There was only one problem: Rick was known as a screamer. He was extremely impatient with mistakes by legal secretaries and paralegals. When those mistakes happened, he quickly lost his temper. He would even yell at himself if he made a mistake on his own. Sarah, a partner in the firm who supervised the associates, was interested in helping Rick. He was a good lawyer who could make the firm more effective. Sarah had often seen bright people whose talents were diluted by impatience. Ideas came fast to those people, and they couldn't understand why others moved slower. In a few minutes, Rick could do crossword puzzles that took most people an hour. But instead of thinking that this was an extraordinary ability on his part, he thought other people were stupid. This was not an endearing characteristic.

When Sarah tried to talk with Rick about his problem, he was defensive at first, but then he agreed to work on his tendency to blow up at people. Sarah suspected that he agreed to this mainly because he didn't want his quick temper to scuttle his legal career, which it could actually have done. She further suspected that Rick would need some patience on her part to become a more patient person himself.

Based on her experience, Sarah knew certain key points that she'd need to stress with Rick. You can use these same points in dealing with anyone who is impatient. You can even use them with yourself.

For example, Sarah continuously reminded Rick of progress he'd made and the effort that he was showing. She emphasized the positive rather than the negative. If Rick had gotten out of line on Monday morning, but had behaved differently on Monday afternoon, Sarah ignored the former and focused on the latter.

She also told Rick to expect setbacks and mistakes. He needed an attitude of "one day at a time." This was difficult for Rick because he wanted everything to happen right away. Sometimes he even blamed Sarah for what he was going through. She wasn't supporting him. She didn't care about him. She didn't understand him. She didn't respect him, and so on and so forth.

At such moments, Sarah pointed out that this was exactly how other people felt about Rick when he was impatient with them. Then she asked Rick to participate in a written exercise that she had devised. At first he resisted and accused Sarah of treating him like a child. But when she reminded him that his future was at stake, he agreed to do what she asked.

The exercise was quite simple. Sarah asked Rick to write down the thoughts and beliefs that occurred to him over a day, as long as they pertained to issues of patience and impatience. Rick gave her this list:

- *I should be able to do things faster and better. So should everybody else.*
- *I shouldn't have to repeat myself. People should understand me the first time.*
- *Why should it take so long and so much effort to change and grow?*
- *I have so much to accomplish. There will be no time to do it all.*
- *There is a right way and a wrong way to do things. Why is it that everyone I come in contact with chooses the wrong way?*
- *It makes no difference how much progress I've made if I haven't accomplished my target goals.*
- *I dislike things such as diets, counseling, and physical therapy. They all take too long.*
- *Since I have to be perfect, everybody else must be perfect. If people are not perfect, it must be because they don't want to be.*

- *I am trying to change, but I see other people falling back into their old habits. That must mean they aren't trying as hard as I am.*

But the last thing Rick wrote was the most telling:

- *I am an impossible case. There is no way that I can ever change.*

Over time, Sarah was able to show Rick how each of the points he'd written was a fundamental misperception, but none of them were as far off the mark as the last one. The reason for this was simple: the only thing Rick definitely *could* change was himself—and until he made that change, everything else was going to stay the same. That's because everything else was not only his *perception,* but also a *projection* of his own problems.

It's odd that impatient people are often so eager to waste time and energy on things they can't control—especially other people. When it comes to patience, the trick is to change yourself. When you do that, you'll be amazed at how different everybody else looks.

In closing this chapter on patience with a purpose, let's bring the focus clearly onto you. To identify the current state of your patience, think about how you would answer the following questions. You might want to write down your responses in a journal or on a piece of paper. You can do that now or later. Or you can just form your answers in your mind.

First, at the start of this chapter we defined patience as follows: *patience is the ability to wait without experiencing anger, anxiety, or frustration.* Are you satisfied with this definition, or can you think of one that works better for you?

Second, on a scale from one to ten, how patient are you when a problem presents itself? Are you more patient at work than in your personal life, or is it the other way around? Can you think of examples in both areas to illustrate your conclusion? If there's a big difference between work and elsewhere, why do you think this is so? What can you do toward equalizing the difference?

Again on a scale from one to ten, how patient are you with yourself in areas of your life that you feel you need to change? Using the same scale, how patient are you with other people? What does this comparison tell you? For example, are you extremely demanding only of yourself? Or do you expect even more from others? Many impatient people have a way of justifying their demands on others. They say that they're equally hard on themselves. It's not surprising that other people often disagree with this assessment. If you feel you can get a candid reply, you might want to ask some coworkers or friends about how this equation plays out for you.

A related question is this: How do others react to your lack of patience with yourself? Or to your lack of patience with them? Have you experienced any negative consequences because of your lack of patience? If so, how did the consequences change your behavior? Or were you determined to remain exactly the same?

What feelings do you experience when you are impatient? Are they pleasant or unpleasant? If they're unpleasant, as they are for most people, why do you think you remain attached to them? What prevents you from letting go of them immediately?

What beliefs block your ability to have patience? For example, do you believe that if you lighten up for a second, everything will fall apart? What reason might you have for a belief like that? How can you test your beliefs about patience? What alternative beliefs could help you to have greater patience both with yourself and with others?

This last question about alternative beliefs is so important that some specific suggestions might be useful. Please take the following to heart:

Accept that everything takes time—and probably more time than you might like. This includes changes you are trying to make in yourself. Be prepared for resistance to changing old ways of acting, reacting, and believing.

Reframe your perspective on the past, present, and future. Don't dwell on what went wrong yesterday as a way of justifying unreasonable expectations today. For the same reason, don't become preoccupied with what might happen tomorrow. Live each new day as a fresh start.

Instead of trying to do everything at once, break down larger goals into short- and medium-term objectives.

Many people who have a problem with patience are like Rick, the young lawyer we mentioned earlier. They think they're so far gone that they're beyond anyone's help, even their own. Can you see how this is a kind of reverse arrogance? It's a backhanded way of saying that you're unique. Don't fall into this way of thinking. You're not the greatest sinner who ever lived. People who were much more problematic than you have made major changes in their lives.

Become sensitive to the realities of other people's lives. They are busy with their own struggles, weaknesses, setbacks, relapses, crises, and obstacles. Your needs are not the only thing people have to think about. What's more, your needs should not be the only thing *you* have to think about either.

IS IT EASY TO LEARN PATIENCE?

The short answer is no. Patience is probably one of the most difficult personal qualities to master. It takes time and energy. But class does not come easy. And it's not supposed to come easy.

We live in a society that values instant gratification. Millions of dollars have been made by companies such as FedEx and Domino's Pizza simply because they address the issue of how long customers will have to wait. Because waiting, in our culture, translates into feeling frustrated, forgotten, stressed-out, and most of all angry. So learning patience has many benefits, although you might need some patience to learn them! Here are some ideas:

Know the difference between the things you control, the things you can influence, and the things over which you have no control or influence. Spend the bulk of your time and attention on the things that you control. This is where you can make the biggest difference. Spend your remaining time and attention on the things you can influence, knowing things may not go your way. Let go of the things over which you have no control or influence. Time or attention spent on those is just wasted.

Live one day at a time. Treat each day as a treasured gift because that is exactly what it is! Yesterday is done and tomorrow has not yet arrived, so make the most of today because it is all you have to work with anyway.

Accept and forgive yourself. You are growing, learning, and changing all the time—or at least you should be. As a human being, even an unforgettable one, you will make mistakes. Get over it and get on with life. Forgive yourself for your mistakes, weaknesses, and imperfections. Learn from them and move on.

Change your point of view. Instead of beating yourself up over past mistakes, accept them as part of who you are today. Class is progress, not perfection.

Plan your life and follow your plan. Have plan B ready in case things do not go the way you expect. Otherwise you're going to set yourself up for frustration. Nothing is more maddening than waiting for the phone to ring! If you're in that position, you'll probably need more patience than you've got. So hope for the best, but prepare for something other than the best, too.

Set big goals, then take baby steps. You can accomplish any goal by breaking it down into doable steps that keep you motivated along the way. Celebrate each time you complete a step toward your goal.

Confront your feelings about not immediately reaching your goals. Remember that the world was not created in one day. The tallest trees start out as little seeds and take years to grow into their strength and beauty. Every step you take brings you closer to the results you desire.

No worries. Worrying about tomorrow saps your energy and strength today. Instead, use that energy to work toward your goals.

Become your own best friend. You are the only person you will live with your entire life, so get to know yourself well and treat yourself as the valuable person you are.

Many years ago the philosopher Reinhold Niebuhr wrote the words that have come to be known as the Serenity Prayer the first two lines of which are:

God, give us grace to accept with serenity
the things that cannot be changed,

Everything we have said in this chapter is expressed in those two lines and the ones that follow. If you sincerely desire to be a more patient person, don't forget them. If you want to be a class act, live in accordance with them. If you want to be an unforgettable person, teach them to other people as well.

CHAPTER TWELVE

Intelligence beyond Intellect

"Intelligence beyond intellect"? What can that possibly mean?

In one word, it means *intuition.* For many people who have made themselves unforgettable, intuition has always been a basic element of their success. To see what this means, let's look at a case in point.

The Walt Disney Company is one of the greatest success stories in the history of American business, and intuition has played an important role in the company from the beginning. When Walt Disney drew his first cartoon mouse, for example, he wanted to call the mouse Mortimer. That didn't sound right to his wife, and she suggested changing it to Mickey. Could she have given a well-thought-out reason why she preferred Mickey? Probably not. Was a marketing survey done to see which name the public preferred. No—because marketing surveys didn't exist at that time, and Walt Disney couldn't have afforded one anyway. But Mortimer was changed to Mickey and the rest, as they say, is history. It all happened because of a hunch on the part of Walt Disney's wife.

Several decades later, Walt Disney put a hunch of his own into action. In 1939 there had been a huge World's Fair in New York City. Millions of people came from all over the world to attend.

The fair was a truly historic occasion, but eventually it was over. Everything was dismantled. Millions of people had come, but what about the millions who might have wanted to come but didn't? What about the people who came but who might have wanted to come back? It was too late for them. The fair was gone forever.

In the mid-1950s, Walt Disney had the idea of creating a version of the World's Fair that would be permanent. People could come as many times as they wanted over several years, or even over a lifetime. No one would have to come to the fair at any specific date, but sooner or later a huge number of people would make the trip. A whole generation would visit, and someday they would bring their own children, and the visits would go on forever.

This was the invention of what has come to be known as the theme park, but at the time it was just a hunch on the part of Walt Disney. He had no feasibility studies or demographic research. He did have access to some land south of Los Angeles, but he had nowhere near enough money to construct the project. Furthermore, no one wanted to make an investment in Walt Disney's hunch. Banks turned it down. It seemed as if the vision would never be realized.

But Disney had an idea for solving this problem. He approached executives of the American Broadcasting Company with a proposition. In return for their investment in the park, Walt Disney would create a one-hour weekly TV show called—what a surprise—*Disneyland.* The show would feature animated cartoons and nature movies of animals from around the world. And here was the best part: each show would also include progress reports on the construction of the park in Southern California. This plan was a huge success—as was Disneyland, from the day it opened in 1955.

It's interesting to note that intelligence as it's generally understood played almost no role in this story. Certainly the investors who rejected the Disneyland concept didn't behave intelligently. If they had, a couple of important things might have occurred to them. They might have noticed that the interstate highway system was being constructed, which would give American families far greater mobility than ever before, and the growth of the airline industry would do the same thing. But this didn't occur to the money managers who turned down Walt Disney's idea. That was a mistake, but it was an even bigger mistake to overlook the immense growth in population that was taking place in the years after the Second World War. Between 1946 and 1964 the baby boom generation was coming into being: more than 70 million children, a huge percentage of whom would sooner or later visit Disneyland. But none of the bankers or investment analysts thought of this, despite their being experienced and highly trained professionals.

Amazingly, Walt Disney didn't think of it either. He wasn't focused on the demographic shifts or the airline industry or the highway system. He just wanted to have a permanent World's Fair—because he hated the idea that previous World's Fairs came to an end. He wanted his permanent World's Fair to have a perfect version of Main Street in a small town—because he hated the idea that the small town of his childhood had vanished. The twist, of course, is that the small town of Walt Disney's childhood had never actually existed, but that's another story. The point is that intellect didn't help the people who rejected Disney's idea, nor was intellect behind the creation of the idea in the first place.

It was just a flash of intuition in Walt Disney's brain, or more likely in his *heart*. It was just a hunch.

Maybe you haven't had an idea like Disneyland yet, but you know the intuitive power that brought it into being. Call it a hunch, a flash of insight, or a sudden inspiration, but how many times have you had a strong feeling—positive or negative—about a job, a coworker, a potential business deal? How many times have you suddenly found the answer to a question you didn't even know you were asking? And if you're like most people, your answer was sometimes correct. There's a good chance you wrote it off to coincidence. But there's also a good chance that you weren't completely satisfied with that explanation.

We all have flashes of intuition, but we ignore or distrust them as irrational and useless distractions. We all have inner capabilities, but we need to give them the value they deserve, no more and no less. In this chapter you'll learn the difference between ignoring your intuitive powers and trusting them blindly. You'll see how to make the most of intuition without making too much of it. You'll learn how to tap into insight beyond conventional intelligence, and you'll see why the ability to do this is an important quality of an unforgettable human being. Intuition is not just a party game. It's a unique form of personal power that deserves your attention.

To see how this works in the real world, let's look at one of the fastest-growing industries in America in the first years of the twenty-first century—namely, the security industry, which provides protection against terrorist attacks for corporate and public locations. By now everyone is familiar with the heightened security checks at airports. But if you've been to New York or another large city lately, you know that gaining entrance to a major office building is every bit as complicated as boarding an airliner. You're required to empty your pockets and pass through metal detectors, and you're issued a pass to the building that expires after a specific time.

Companies in the security industry have invested a great deal of thought and money on ways to simplify this process. Millions of dollars would be made by any firm that could come up with a mechanical or electronic search technology that's fast and reliable. Many ingenious methods are being tried, including palm prints, voice analyzers, and even dogs that are trained to smell fear or anger.

But all these techniques have one problem. Just as smart people are coming up with new security technologies, smart people are also figuring out ways to beat them. Many of the best thinkers on how to beat security checks are employed by the security companies themselves. They're constantly looking for ways to beat the most advanced electronic devices. What's more, those ways always exist. Any device can be beaten—and it only has to be beaten once.

With all the technologies that have been introduced, only one security screening system cannot consistently be beaten if it is properly employed. That system is a trained and focused human being, and preferably more than one of them. Potential attackers may be able to penetrate the most carefully constructed barriers, but they can still be tripped up by the intuition of a diligent man or woman. In an industry that's become lucrative and high-tech, the last and best line of defense is still a person's eyes and ears.

Consider this. Suppose you wanted to build a machine that could duplicate the performance of an outfielder in major league baseball. The machine would need some advanced mechanical and electronic capabilities. It would need to detect and track a line drive leaving a bat. It would have to instantly calculate the point where the ball will hit the ground. It will then have to move quickly toward that point to catch the ball. Then the machine will have to throw the ball toward home plate on exactly the correct trajectory. The path of the ball has to be just right, so that the runner can be tagged out before he scores.

Leaving aside the mechanical challenges in building such a machine, it would certainly require a team of mathematicians and physicists just to look at all the various arcs and angles.

But Mickey Mantle was not a mathematician. Willie Mays was not a computer scientist. Neither of those ballplayers stopped to logically consider what he was doing when he made a throw from the outfield. They performed extremely complex operations by instinct, not reason or intelligence. They felt how to catch a ball.

They felt how to throw it. If you asked them how they did it, they couldn't have told you. But they could certainly show you.

A leading business school studied two thousand CEOs whose companies had doubled their profits in the past five years. Eighty percent of these executives reported that they relied on intuitive approaches to reach important decisions. They studied all relevant information and available data, but they still came to conclusions based on factors that could not be quantified.

So often the best decision is a hunch that defies logic. It's an inner feeling or flash of insight that brings the optimal solution. Professionals who are both rational thinkers and highly intuitive decision-makers do best in the real world. They have a distinct advantage in meeting challenges and solving problems. As you'll learn, you can take clear steps to join their number.

Let's imagine three examples of people who have very different approaches to decision-making. Our first person, we'll call him Steve, has an uncritical orientation to the world, which he likes to think is intuition. Steve says:

"I don't need to spend a lot of time thinking things over. I trust my gut. Some people are very intelligent, but they're too smart for their own good. They overthink everything. I have a sixth sense that leads me in the right direction—and if it leads me in the wrong direction and I get into trouble, I still trust my sixth sense to get me out."

Steve does not see any reason to intellectualize his life. He tells himself that he trusts his gut, but somehow his gut usually leads him down the path of least resistance. Actually, he's pretty much taking things as they come. As a result, Steve can be vulnerable to more sophisticated, manipulative individuals. His passive approach sometimes makes him seem helpless and inadequate, but also likable in a childlike way. This can cause other people to do things for Steve, perhaps because they feel sorry for him.

Our second example is named Laurie. She has a very different approach:

"When I need to make a decision, I think about it for as long as I possibly can. I especially focus on the things that can go wrong when I look at a certain course of action. Sometimes my careful thinking about various options takes so long that the options have disappeared by the time I make a decision. But maybe that's what I wanted to happen in the first place. I guess I'm really more comfortable with thought than with action. I may miss some good opportunities, but at least I avoid some bad mistakes."

Laurie values logical thinking, and the more she does it, the more she values it. As even she admits, she often values thinking above acting. Laurie's is a classic case of what Zig Ziglar calls "paralysis by analysis."

Our third person is named Brian. He says:

"I try to think carefully about my decisions, but sometimes I still do things impulsively. If something is really a close call and I don't know which way to go, I may even flip a coin to make the decision. Or maybe I'll just go with the route that seems best at the moment. If a decision really seems to be so equally balanced on both sides, probably the most important thing is to follow through on the choice you make. There will be advantages and disadvantages on both sides, so the best thing is to realize that you won't be completely happy or unhappy. You just try to feel comfortable with the result that comes about."

Brian is an interesting contrast to both Laurie and Steve. Like Laurie, Brian values the power of rational thinking. But unlike Laurie, that's not *all* he values. Brian also resembles Steve in the importance he gives to his gut feelings, but he doesn't let that translate into fatalism and passivity. Brian knows the limits of both logic and intuition. He tries to use both of them, but he also knows that at times neither will give him a hard-and-fast answer. That's when you have to make the best decision you can, then live with the decision that you have made. A class act knows that at times things won't work out as well as hoped. When that happens, unforgettable people know how to make the best of it.

They also trust that things will happen differently next time. And sometimes things will not only happen differently, but in ways you never expected.

Here's an example. In the 1960s, James Watson and Francis Crick were two young research biologists at Cambridge University in England. They were struggling to understand the molecular structure of DNA, the genetic code that is the basis of life on earth. This was one of the most important questions in the history of science. Watson and Crick explored many different possibilities for the structure of DNA, but none of them proved correct. So they kept trying. It was hugely frustrating, but they didn't give up.

Then one night Francis Crick had a dream about a coiled snake. When he woke up, he thought about the dream, and he saw that the snake had revealed a new idea for the molecular structure. Incredibly, when Crick and Watson tested the idea, it proved correct. After years of intellectual work, the solution came in the intuitive wisdom of a single dream. The world was changed, and Watson and Crick won a Nobel Prize.

But one crucial fact needs to be understood. Crick would never have had that dream if he hadn't been thinking so hard about the problem. It was no coincidence that a dream about the structure of DNA came to him rather than someone else. He had paid his dues in terms of conscious thought. This is where the "class" aspect of this story reveals itself. Having the dream was not a class act, but becoming the person who would have it definitely was. By making such a sustained effort over such a long time, Crick's unconscious energy was mobilized. The electricity was always in the wall. He just had to make himself ready for flipping the switch.

You can make yourself ready, too, and developing your intuition is not as difficult as it may seem. We all have it and it's always working, even without any effort on our part. The force is within us, constantly yearning to be expressed. We just have to prepare ourselves so that intuition can reveal itself. Then we need to recognize the power that's been given to us and use it well. It's all a matter of seeing the importance of intuition, without thinking that intuition is the only thing that's important.

Developing your intuition means accessing intuitive information in an unblocked form—without interruption, confusion, or rational analysis, which can get in the way. In everyday life, we're trained to be logical and objective. We're cautioned to be suspicious of ideas that can't be verified. We come to believe that everything can be explained reasonably and scientifically. If you stop there, you can be an intelligent person. But you'll never be an *inspired* person. You may be in touch with all the many things that logic can explain, but you won't connect with the things that are beyond logic.

Valuing your intuition is easy to start. The next time you get a phone call, take a second before you answer. Ask yourself who might be on the other end of the line. Try to do this quickly. Don't let the phone keep ringing while you stand there running through the possibilities. Just quickly make a mental inquiry and see what pops into your head. It may not even be a name. It could be the memory of an incident that involved a certain person. It could be the image of an object that's associated with a particular individual.

The telephone isn't the only way to practice intuitive thinking. Keeping a journal is probably the most valuable exercise of all. But before you run out and buy a spiral notebook, be aware that worthwhile journaling isn't easy. It takes discipline to fill up a page or two every day, and then you'll need to reflect on what you've written to see what insights occur to you. Remember, Francis Crick would not have dreamed the structure of DNA if he had not worked so hard first. Or, if he had dreamed it, he would not have understood it. So mentally prepare yourself quickly for writing a journal the same way you would prepare for any other significant task, because if you don't do the preparation, the task won't be significant.

Use your journal to capture your ideas, observations, and perceptions. Write down dreams, feelings, and hunches. If you have a business meeting tomorrow with people you haven't met, guess how they'll look and how they'll approach the business they plan to conduct. Record flashes of insight and keep a record of decisions you make on that basis. Check back occasionally to see which of your hunches were correct. By keeping score, you'll be able to evaluate your accuracy and possibly increase it.

As you practice the exercises on intuition, remember that you're working toward awakening certain faculties in yourself that may have been dormant for a long time. Don't be discouraged if results fail to show up immediately. Make a continuous effort, and you could be amazed by the results.

Making the connection between intuition and intellect doesn't have to be difficult. Chances are, the connection already exists in your mind and heart. But here's an important point. Most people have it *backward.* They're trying to write with the wrong end of the pencil. They're trying to start the car by turning off the engine. Worst of all, they probably don't even know it!

Most people are convinced that *first and foremost* they have to deal with the material issues in their lives. For instance, they have to get *rich*! They have to get money in the bank! They have to get the car, the house, and the trust fund. Then, and not before, they'll be ready to deal with the intangible elements of their lives. They think the intangibles are the warm and fuzzy part. The material things are the rock-solid realities. They value one side above the other. But it shouldn't be a matter of picking one side over the other. It's much more important to value both sides of yourself—the inside and the outside—and get them working together.

We want to take care of the outside first, and secondly we'll take care of the inside. So what happens? We work and work to get greater responsibilities, more prestigious titles, and most of all we work to get *more money.* We think that once that's accomplished, everything else will fall into place. This is a mistake. The foundation of success isn't that the inside comes before the outside—or the other way around. Being a class act isn't a matter of feeling over intellect or of mind over heart. Making yourself unforgettable means all the parts of yourself are working together.

In closing this chapter, here's a story to keep in mind. A young man named Bob was determined to get in touch with his inner inspirational powers. He meditated intensely to develop his intuition. He wanted to be able to see into the future, but he wasn't doing this just for fun. He was determined to win the lottery by using his intuition. But week after week he was disappointed.

One day Bob went out for a cup of coffee with a close friend. During their conversation, Bob talked about the way his intuition was letting him down. "I get such a strong picture of which number is going to win," he said, "and it never seems to happen. I know that intuition is a hugely powerful force, and I'm doing everything I possibly can to harness it. What do I have to do to win the lottery?"

Bob was obviously in tremendous emotional pain. His friend looked at him for a moment, then said, "Bob, maybe it would help if you bought a ticket."

THE LIMITS OF INTUITION

We've seen that you probably know more than you think. But that doesn't mean you know everything!

A big mistake on the part of many executives and managers is meeting with clients while having a preconceived idea of what the other people need. The first step in learning what people want is to ask them. While some of your clients and team members may have a superficial notion of what their business needs, others have really wrestled with the issue, and they have a pretty in-depth idea of what they need from you.

Earlier, we devoted an entire chapter to the importance of listening. Sometimes listening to what people tell you will reveal avenues to serving their needs. Listening closely may help you uncover other underlying needs of which the people are not even consciously aware. But if you enter a meeting with clients and suggest that you understand their business needs better than the clients do—well, you shouldn't expect to get far.

Let's look at this issue strictly within a business context. Another way to learn client needs is to look at relevant industry-related blogs and forums to see what problems other companies within the field are experiencing. This will give you a greater knowledge and understanding of your clients' business. The more you know what they are facing, the better able you will be to provide them with what they really need.

Unless you are fortunate enough to be in a unique niche, other companies are probably providing a similar product or service to yours. To learn what your clients are looking for, see what your competition is providing. Some companies spend significant revenue on researching the needs of their clients, and you may be able to piggyback on their efforts. Look at what these companies are providing, and if necessary adapt your product offering to make sure you are truly competitive.

Many times providing one service or product will open opportunities to provide more services. As you build trust with your clients, they may be more willing to listen to suggestions or may even ask your opinion on what other things you could provide. You may be in a position to offer related services that were not previously considered, or that were being provided by another company. Those new opportunities could in turn lead to even more opportunities.

The key to learning client needs starts with a willingness to truly listen to what clients have to say. The more you listen and learn, the more you will be able to offer suggestions, and to lead them to the root of their needs.

And the more you do that, the more unforgettable you will be.

CHAPTER THIRTEEN

Resilience without Regret

Resilience is a word that is finding an increasing number of uses in the modern world. Resilience is the ability to recover from and successfully adapt to adversity. Psychiatrists and educators often use the word in discussing children who have experienced dysfunctional families or other forms of trauma. Environmentalists speak of the resilience of a region that has been subjected to droughts or major storms.

Resilience has also become a hot word in business and corporate circles. In less turbulent times, executives could assume that business models would pretty much last forever. Companies always worked to get better, but they seldom worked to become different. They didn't need to rethink their essential reason for being. But today fundamental change is essential, not only for companies as a whole but also for the human beings comprised by them. Collectively and individually, success no longer hinges on momentum or market share. It demands resilience—the power to dynamically reinvent yourself as circumstances change.

In this sense, resilience is more than responding to a onetime crisis or rebounding from a setback. It's about continually anticipating and adjusting to shifting trends. Companies, people, and perhaps even nations that don't change are bound to quickly lose influence. This presents some challenges for all of us, but resilience seems to be an innate human capacity. The ability to bounce back is stronger in some people than in others, but you can strengthen your resilience just as you can build up your muscles or your bank account. Creating that strength is essential for anyone who aspires to be a class act. Class is the ability to find extra energy when it's needed. Further, class means finding *even more* extra energy after the reserves have been used up. Research shows that to some extent this is an inherent capacity. Your responsibility is to maximize that capacity in your life every day.

In doing this, the first step is self-assessment. Research shows that certain conditions in people's lives help them to be resilient. Listen to the following ten groups of questions and answer yes or no. The more times you answer yes, the more resources you have to recover strongly from problems and setbacks. When you answer no, think about what changes you need to make and how you plan to make them.

1. Do you have several people in your life who give you unconditional love and nonjudgmental listening, people who will be "there for you" even in difficult times?

2. Are you involved in a school, a company, a spiritual organization, or other group where you feel cared for and valued? Do you feel an emotional connection with a number of people in your work or your professional life?

3. Are you in good health and decent physical condition? Do you avoid unhealthy food and drink? Are you getting enough sleep and exercise?

4. Do you have people in your life who believe in your ability to survive, to succeed, and to prosper? Do you get

encouragement and positive reinforcement from these people regularly?

5. Regardless of what others may think, do you have faith in *yourself*? Do you feel generally optimistic about your ability to accomplish your goals—even when you encounter problems?

6. Do you feel that your opinions and your decisions are heard and valued in your close personal relationships?

7. Are your ideas listened to, respected, and frequently accepted in your work and career?

8. Do you volunteer to help others in your community and in the world? This can mean donating your time through a community or spiritual organization, or making regular charitable financial donations.

9. Do most of your relationships with friends and family members have clear boundaries—providing mutual respect, personal independence, and both giving and receiving on the part of each person? Do you set and maintain boundaries for yourself by saying no when you need to?

10. Are you a generally optimistic person? Do you believe things tend to work out for the best?

If you answered yes to a majority of those questions, you seem to have a strong support system in various areas of your life. You have people and organizations you can rely on when you need them. Along with external resources, people also overcome difficulties through internal qualities. What follows can be thought of as a "personal resiliency list." Probably no one possesses all the elements on this list. You may have three or four of these qualities that you use most naturally and most often. Still, you may never have clearly identified these attributes in your mind. It's useful to recognize your primary resiliency builders, and it's also important to develop new ones to the greatest possible extent.

There are seven personal resiliency builders. As you hear each one described, ask yourself whether it's a strong presence in your life, just average, or a relatively weak area that you could probably develop.

We can call the first quality sociability. How good are you at being a friend and in forming positive relationships?

The second trait is humor. This doesn't mean you tell jokes all the time. It's means seeing the comical element in life. It also means being able to laugh at yourself even in serious circumstances.

The third trait is insight. Do you think you have above average understanding of people and situations? Do you feel that you often see things that others miss?

Number four is called adaptive distancing. Are you generally able to recognize negative people and situations, and to keep your distance from them?

The fifth trait is flexibility. How well do you adjust to change? Are you able to bend but not break in challenging situations?

Trait six is personal competence. Is there something that you're really good at, something that gives you renewed self-confidence and energy?

The seventh trait, which is probably the most important of all in terms of resilience, is perseverance. How well are you able to keep on trying despite difficulty? Do you tend give up pretty quickly? Or slowly? Or never?

We've presented quite a few questions so far in this chapter. If you've answered them thoughtfully, you should have an accurate assessment of your external and internal sources of resiliency. That's only the beginning. Now you need to develop the resources you have and initiate the ones you don't have. The time to do that is *now.* Anticipation is probably the most important resiliency builder of all. Recognizing that things could go wrong is important, but it's not much help if it doesn't motivate action.

So please listen closely. Here are seven ways to build resilience, both during a crisis and before the crisis occurs—in other words, right now.

First, make connections. Meet new people—meet as many of them as you can. Don't be judgmental about it. Don't find a way to cancel a lunch with a friend of a friend just because you don't see how that person can be of help to you. On the contrary, that's a good reason for going through with the meeting. You don't see how people can help you, but after you meet them, your eyes might be opened. Or maybe they can't help you now, but when conditions change, that fact might change, too. Finally, there's always the possibility that a class act such as *you* might be able to help *them.* You might be able to make yourself unforgettable.

Second, avoid seeing a crisis as an insurmountable problem. Don't catastrophize. Quick—think back to what you were worried about two years ago. Was it as terrible as it seemed? Did the world end, or are you still here? What about three years ago? Can you even remember? What does that tell you?

Third, accept that change, both positive and negative, is part of living. Flexibility is the key, especially since what looks negative today might look very different tomorrow. You've probably heard the song about poker: "Every hand's a winner, and every hand's a loser." The mark of a class act is knowing how to play a bad hand. With the exception of a genuine tragedy, virtually everything in life has an upside to it. Resilience means surviving the downside, then recognizing the upside and taking advantage of it. Is it easy? No—and it's not supposed to be easy.

Fourth, move steadily and consistently toward your goals even in the face of adversity, and also take decisive action right now to bring the adversity to an end. When Thomas Watson was the head of IBM, nothing riled him as much as inaction during a crisis. Once he walked into a meeting of his top executives and found that they were waiting for him to arrive before they made any decisions. Watson was furious. "Do anything—but do something!" he announced. "If you do the right thing, that's wonderful. And if you do the wrong thing, we'll fix it!"

Fifth, look for self-discovery opportunities. Picture this: Your small daughter wants a new dollhouse for Christmas. She begs, she pleads, she cries. How can you resist—you get her the dollhouse. It's expensive, but that's not the big surprise. The big surprise is that you've got to put it together. There are about five hundred parts, and your daughter watches patiently—or impatiently—as you try to figure out where each one goes. The task takes six or seven hours. What have you learned at the end of the day? An average person might say, "I learned how to put together a dollhouse." A class act would say, "I learned that I have much more patience than I ever imagined."

Next, keep things in perspective. Imagine that you're swimming in the ocean about twenty yards from shore. Suddenly you feel a powerful current pulling you out to sea. It's a riptide, also known as an undertow. What are you going to do? Most people start fighting against the current, which is hopeless of course, because the water is a lot heavier and stronger than any human being. Each year this leads to a number of drownings as people wear themselves out and eventually go under. As any lifeguard will tell you, the correct thing to do is just relax and let the riptide do its thing. It's not going to take you all the way to China. Maybe it will take you another thirty yards out. So what? Then you can swim back in. By that time—unless you've been foolish enough to swim on a deserted beach—someone will see what's happening and get you help. It's all just a matter of keeping your head. Don't overreact. Things are not as bad as they seem, unless you make them even worse!

Finally, make sure you get enough rest, food, support, and even laughter. In short, take care of yourself. Even in a crisis, make time for things that you enjoy and find relaxing. Physical exercise is especially important. Taking care of yourself helps to keep your mind and body ready to deal with a situation that demands resilience.

The best ways to build resiliency will vary from one person to another. The key is to identify ideas that are likely to work well for you. So far we've looked at tactical actions you can take when a crisis strikes, or when you know there's a good chance of that happening. In a moment we'll look at the deeper foundations on which resiliency is built.

When people become overwhelmed by adversities, the result can be depressed thoughts and self-destructive actions. Usually there are clues when this starts to happen, although often the clues are overlooked—even by the person who is creating them. When people are feeling pain, they may feel shame about it. This can cause them to try to hide their emotions, or to present them in guarded ways. So be alert when you hear statements like the following, and be especially alert if you hear yourself making them.

"There seem to be a lot more problems than solutions."

"I feel like things are getting out of control."

"I feel like I can't really change whatever is going on in my life."

"I'm not sure I really care anymore."

And the granddaddy of them all, which we referred to in a previous chapter: "What's the use?"

If you are having feelings like this, it doesn't mean you're not a class act. It does mean you're in crisis, and you need access to some resilience. Sometimes the problem may be so well established that professional help is needed. Most often, however, a lot can be done by people on their own. As we've mentioned, the sooner the foundations of resilience are laid, the better off you'll be.

Many people have not had the opportunity to develop the building blocks of resilience. Fortunately, it is not too late to do that now, and a good way to make yourself unforgettable is to help someone with that. People can learn to respond to obstacles with resilience rather than depression.

This requires creating a foundation for resilience using five building blocks: *trust, independence, initiative, energy,* and *identity.* Let's look at them one by one.

Trust means believing in and relying on other people. Trust begins at birth, and it either strengthens or weakens as life goes on. At first, we have no choice but to trust others to feed and protect us. If that trust is not fulfilled by other people, the trusting impulse weakens—and now we have a choice. We can choose not to trust the people in our lives, or the world as a whole, and we can even choose not to trust ourselves.

When trust is weak or absent in someone, several things can begin to happen, and none of them are good for that individual, for his or her employer, or for you if you are a colleague or a manager of that person.

For example, if people feel they can't trust themselves to achieve and succeed, they may try to protect themselves from their inevitable failure. They may become dependent. They may want you to do things for them because they assume you're better than they are and you'll protect them. Or they may go in the other direction and become dominant and aggressive.

Chances are that you've dealt with someone who has a controlling personality. Someone who seems determined to tell everybody what to do, how to do it, when to do it, and so on. This kind of personality is clearly based on a lack of trust. It comes from seeing everyone as incompetent, hostile, and maybe even dangerous. In effect, a controlling person says, "To keep you from failing me, and maybe even harming me, I have to control you."

The problem, however, is that total control of the physical and human environment is impossible. So controlling people have to become more and more controlling. When they fail, they lack resilience because they have put all their eggs in the basket of control and it didn't work. Game over.

So the ability to trust is a fundamental building block of resilience. It is in your self-interest, and the interest of your organization, to help people find trust. As a class act, you have an opportunity to give them this important building block. How can you do that? It's simple and logical. You help other people develop trust by being trustworthy yourself. You do that by being reliable, by respecting each individual, by not betraying confidences, and in dozens of other ways. Then, once you've established trusting relationships with people, you can help them develop skills they can use to find others they can trust. You've become an unforgettable person in people's eyes, and now you can show them how to find other unforgettable people.

Remember this simple formula: the way to become trusting is by bringing trustworthy people into your life. The way to help other people develop trust is to be trustworthy yourself.

A second building block of resilience is *independence*: the *desire* to make your own decisions in both good times and bad, and the *power* to make the right decisions more often than not. There's an interesting paradox here. Independence becomes stronger with success, but it also depends on failure. You can't become resilient if you've never failed. You can't learn to get up off your back if you've never been knocked down. You can't become independent if you've always had someone taking care of you.

Imagine that you're the parent of a daughter who takes her homework seriously. If she gets a poor grade on an assignment, she gets terribly upset. Naturally, you want to protect her—and yourself—from having to deal with this. So you start helping her with her homework. Pretty soon you're not just helping her anymore, you're actually doing the assignments yourself. Although your intentions were good—you wanted to protect her—the outcome can be problematic. She lacks independence for the simple reason that she's dependent on you. She lacks resilience because she's never learned to come back from failure.

To establish the building block of independence, reinforce success—but don't avoid failure at all cost. The cost can be much higher than you anticipated.

Building block number three is *initiative*—the ability and willingness to take action. We spoke a moment ago about the problem of failure avoidance in developing independence. This is an important factor in initiative as well. The key to this building block is detachment from the outcome of an action. You need to stop thinking in terms of a successful or unsuccessful result. If you make an honest attempt and give your best effort, *that in itself* is success.

The United States was founded on the idea of the second chance. People came here from all over the world for two reasons: because things had not gone well for them where they were, and because the new country offered them a chance to start over. It didn't matter what had happened in the past as long as you had the resilience to make another try. In striving to become a resilient person, not to mention a class act, it's absolutely essential to maintain this perspective.

Our fourth building block is *energy*. With respect to resilience, energy comes in two varieties. Let's call the first one inspiration. Suppose your business goes bankrupt. Suppose your investments go bust. Suppose a tornado comes and blows down your house. For a few moments you feel daunted, but then something comes over you. You're determined to get back on your feet. You think of all the great people who have faced even greater problems than you, and you're determined to be like them. You've hooked into a specific energy of resilience, and you go for it. That's inspiration.

Now here's another scenario. You look at that hole in the ground where your house used to be—before the tornado blew it down. Instead of feeling inspired and energetic, you just feel tired and defeated. That age-old question begins to appear in your thoughts: "What's the use?" So how do you respond? If you're a class act, if you're a resilient person, if you're determined to make yourself unforgettable, you fight back *even though you don't feel like it.* Somehow you find the energy even at the very moment that you're asking yourself, "What's the use?" Anybody can accomplish great things when he or she is all charged up and filled with determination. But genuinely resilient people accomplish great things even when they feel far from great themselves. That's not inspiration, that's the force of *will.* To be a resilient human being, you'll want to have both forms of energy—both inspiration and will. Because when the first one is missing, the second one had better be ready to go.

The fifth and last building block of resilience is *identity.* Let's define this through a historical example. Almost twenty-five hundred years ago, Alexander the Great brought his army into Asia to confront the Persian empire, which at that time was the most powerful empire in the world. Alexander's army was much smaller than the Persians', not as well equipped, and his soldiers were fighting far from their homeland. The night before the climactic battle, Alexander stood up to address his troops. Like Joe Namath before the New York Jets played Baltimore in the Super Bowl, Alexander began by guaranteeing victory. Then he said, "Let me give you three reasons why I'm guaranteeing victory. First, we as a nation come from many generations of tough, hardworking people. The enemy, on the other hand, has been taking it easy in their big empire while we were herding sheep and trying to farm the rocky soil of Greece. Second, on an individual basis, we come from tough, hardworking families. Each of you soldiers had a father and a mother who got up in the morning and did what needed to be done. But the families of the enemy are rich and lazy. They sleep late. They don't raise sheep. They are sheep. Now, the final reason we're going to win is the simplest and the most important. The enemy has the ruler of the Persian empire as their leader. But you've got me."

The whole purpose of this speech was to create identity.

Alexander told his troops that they were fundamentally different and fundamentally better than the enemy. He gave them things they could identify with: their nation, their families, and their leader. In the difficult situation that they were facing, they had that identity to support them and to fall back on.

Give some thought to your own identity. What are the points of identification that make you feel confident that things will go well, and more resilient if they don't? When you're working with other people, seek out their sources of identification, and if they don't have any, help them build some. And by the way, Alexander's army did win the battle. It was the greatest upset until the Jets won the Super Bowl.

When something goes wrong, how much class do you have? Will you bounce back or fall apart? Resilience is the ability to harness inner strengths and rebound more quickly from a setback or a challenge, whether it's a job loss, an illness, a disaster, or the death of a loved one.

Lacking resilience, however, you tend to dwell on problems, feel victimized, become overwhelmed, or even turn to reactive behaviors such as substance abuse. You may even be more inclined to develop mental health problems.

Resilience won't make your problems go away, but it can give you the ability to see past them, find enjoyment in life, and handle stress better. If you aren't as resilient as you'd like to be, you can develop skills to become more resilient. It's the ability to roll with the punches. It means that although you encounter stress, adversity, trauma, or tragedy, you keep functioning, both psychologically and physically.

Resilience isn't about toughing it out or living by old clichés such as "grin and bear it." It doesn't mean you ignore your feelings. When adversity strikes, you still experience anger, grief, and pain, but you're able to go on with daily tasks, remain generally optimistic, and go on with your life. Being resilient also doesn't mean being stoic or going it alone. Being able to reach out to others for support is a key component of being resilient.

To strengthen your resilience, try out these ideas:

- Get connected. Build strong, positive relationships with family and friends who provide support and acceptance. Volunteer, get involved in your community, or join a faith or spiritual community.

- Find meaning. Develop a sense of purpose for your life. Having something meaningful to focus on can help you share emotions, feel gratitude, and experience an enhanced sense of well-being.

- Start laughing. Finding humor in stressful situations doesn't mean you're in denial. Humor is a helpful coping mechanism. If you can't find any humor in a situation, turn to other sources for a laugh, such as a funny book or a movie.

- Learn from experience. Think back on how you've coped with hardships in the past. Build on skills and strategies that helped you through the rough times, and don't repeat those that didn't help.

- Remain hopeful. You can't change what's happened in the past, but you can always look toward the future. Find something in each day that signals a change for the better. Expect good results.

- Take care of yourself. Tend to your needs and feelings, both physically and emotionally. This includes participating in activities and hobbies you enjoy, exercising regularly, getting plenty of sleep, and eating well.

- Keep a journal. Write about your experiences, thoughts, and feelings. Journaling can help you experience strong emotions you may otherwise be afraid to unleash. It can also help you see situations in a new way and help you identify patterns in your behavior and reactions.

- Accept and anticipate change. Expecting changes to occur makes it easier to adapt to them, tolerate them, and even welcome them. With practice, you can learn to be more flexible and not view change with as much anxiety.

- Work toward a goal. Do something every day that gives you a sense of accomplishment. Even small, everyday goals are important. Having goals helps you look toward the future.

- Take action. Don't just wish your problems would go away or try to ignore them. Instead, figure out what needs to be done, make a plan, and take action.

- Maintain perspective. Look at your situation in the larger context of your life and of the world. Keep a long-term perspective and know that your situation can improve if you actively work at it.

- Practice stress-management and relaxation techniques. Restore inner peace and calm by practicing yoga, meditation, deep breathing, visualization, imagery, prayer, or muscle relaxation.

The title of this chapter is "Resilience without Regret." That means don't regret your mistakes because you can learn from them. Don't regret obstacles you encounter because you can turn them into opportunities. Resilience and regret are polar opposites. Like light and darkness, they can't coexist. So the choice is yours. As a class act, you'll make the right one.

CHAPTER FOURTEEN

Appreciation beyond the Comfort Zone

Whether we realize it or not, laws of giving and receiving play important roles in our lives. Make no mistake: the ideas we'll be exploring in this chapter are *laws*, not just opinions or sentiments. Ignoring these laws is just as foolish as trying to drive your car after letting the air out of its tires. You can try it, but you won't get far.

More than two hundred years ago, the economic philosopher Adam Smith made a simple statement, but it's still being discussed and argued about. Adam Smith said that society works best when people act in their self-interest. It may surprise you to learn that Dale Carnegie's philosophy agrees with that statement, provided that self-interest is accurately defined and understood. Because *self-interest* is not the same thing as *selfishness*. Self-interest is the opposite of selfishness, as you're about to discover.

It's easy to see why people do selfish things. A man finds someone's wallet on a bus. The wallet has money in it. Like everyone else, the man wants more money than he has at the moment, so he pockets the money from the wallet and throws the wallet in the trash. Whatever you may think of this from an ethical perspective, there's a clear logic to it. Yet sometimes, and more often than you might think, the man will return the money. Keeping it for himself can be explained in one sentence, but returning it takes a little more time. Keeping the money might seem to be in the man's self-interest, but that isn't so simple either.

Why do people do appreciative things? They give help to strangers, they contribute to charities, volunteer in hospitals, send food and supplies to earthquake victims. We describe these acts as charitable or altruistic, rather than self-interested. In contrast, most of our interactions with people involve giving in order to get. We sell goods and services to get money, for example. But appreciation means providing something without the clear expectation of a definite return.

Let me show you why appreciation and self-interest aren't so different after all. It all depends on how we define self-interest. Is it just the satisfaction of short-term desire for material gain? Or is self-interest more than that? Most people have long-term goals beyond just making a quick profit, or even beyond making money at all. They may still be acting out of self-interest, but not in material terms.

Suppose a traveler runs out of gas on a dark country road. A farmer comes by in a jeep. The farmer has a can of gas. He stops and puts gas in the car of the stranded driver. When the driver offers money to the farmer, the farmer shakes his head. "I know what it's like to be stuck on a dark road," he says, "so here's the only payment I ask. Someday you'll see somebody stranded just like you were. When that happens, I want you to stop and help just like I stopped for you now."

Was the farmer acting like a completely irrational person? Would it have been more reasonable to say, "All right, that'll cost you ten bucks." Not at all, because each of us benefits from living in a society where we appreciatively help each other. People act appreciatively partly because the appreciation will someday be extended to them. A young man giving his seat on a bus to an older woman provides a model for that woman, for everyone on the bus. Hopefully, the woman will remember the appreciation she received, and someday she'll help someone else. It will be like repaying a debt.

And what if you don't repay the debt? People who benefit from appreciation but don't extend it are freeloaders. They've taken but they haven't given. People like that are not uncommon in the world. Do they feel bad about themselves? Not always—because there's a simple way to justify their behavior. They say, "Nobody ever gave me anything, so I don't have to give anything back. I haven't received appreciation, so I don't have to offer it."

This is absolutely false. How can people who get out of bed every morning into a new day assert that they've never received anything? How can people who can see with their eyes and hear with their ears believe that they've never received something for nothing—the most appreciative gift possible? The really odd thing is that people who have less are much more likely to honor the gift of life than people who have much more. The more we have, the more we want, and the less we appreciate what's already ours.

This is especially true with money. Money is the medium through which appreciation is most often expressed—or *not* expressed. Absolutely nothing else will bring all our issues to the surface like money. Is money the root of all evil? Well, money and also the *desire* for money have brought a lot of excitement into people's lives—often the kind of excitement they could have done without. Money is the number one source of problems between husbands and wives. It can make trouble between friends, too, and it's an ongoing issue between employer and employee. Money is used to control in various ways—who is giving, who is getting, and what does that mean in terms of the relationship?

Money makes many people uncomfortable. Income is one of the last things people want to disclose about themselves. If they don't make much money, they're ashamed of it, and if they make a lot of money, maybe they're ashamed of that, too.

Money and our relationship to it can be complicated and

confusing. To be a class act, you need to sort this out, because money and how you handle it are some of the most visible expressions of your character and personality. An essential paradox about money has to be understood. On the one hand, money is inherently *limited*: you can't pay for a $20,000 car with a $10,000 check. In that sense, the value of money is clear and straightforward.

But money is also inherently *unlimited*, at least in terms of its potential. Ten dollars may be $10 today, but it can be $20 tomorrow, or even $20,000. Or it can also be no dollars at all. Money is undefined. It is raw, unmanifested energy—it can be used for virtually any purpose, for good or bad.

For lots of people, money is security. This is a hugely important use of people's income. It's also one of the hardest to understand. After all, some people with millions of dollars are still worried about their financial security. Millionaires have been known to commit suicide because they've lost half their fortune. A person could still have a huge net worth, but if it's only half of what it was before, he feels threatened. He feels vulnerable. He just can't go on. Yet he still has more money than the vast majority of the population.

The secret is that money, in and of itself, has no particular value. Money has the value that we give it. Picture a wealthy businessman pulling up at a tollbooth in his gigantic SUV. He tosses in his fifty-cents toll, but he accidentally overshoots the bucket with his quarters. Well, no problem—he just throws in two more. Retrieving the fifty cents is not worth his time and effort. But if a homeless person comes along and finds the fifty cents, that's a major windfall. For one person, any given amount may be meaningless, but to another it's half of all they have. Money has no set value in and of itself. How you *perceive* money is how you value it. *You* actually decide the value of money.

If you don't understand this, it can get you into serious trouble. But once you do understand it, you can make money your willing servant rather than your tyrannical master.

When you prosper in your career, you make money. You earn a profit. That is one of the purposes of business—but it is not the only purpose. Amazing as it may seem, it's not even the most important purpose for a person who wants to be a class act. Because when it comes to class, what you do with your profit is at least as important as earning it in the first place. The most important thing you can do with your profit is to be appreciative with it—give it away, not foolishly but appreciatively. The most important thing is to circulate your money, because it will circulate back to you—maybe not in the form of dollars and cents, but it will reappear in some shape or form. As the Bible says, "Cast your bread upon the waters. You shall find it after many days." Those are some of the wisest words ever written about money and about appreciation.

For most people, appreciation does not come naturally, or easily. But doing what's difficult is what class is all about. To help you confront the difficulties of appreciation, here are six principles to keep in mind. They are definitely informational, and I hope they're inspirational as well. By the time you've listened to the last one, you should understand why giving is really a precondition for getting—and why looking out for the interests of others is actually self-interest in the true meaning of the term.

First, put aside forever the common lament that I mentioned earlier: "Nobody ever did anything for me, so I'm not going to do anything for anybody else." If you live in the United States in the twenty-first century, you should automatically disqualify yourself from that line of thinking. You should do it for your own good. Research shows that a sense of gratitude is the most widely shared emotion among joyful and successful people.

No matter who you are, there are *always* things to be grateful for, so exercise that option. Throughout human history, wherever tyranny has reigned, one of its main goals was to get people focused exclusively on self-interest. In the concentration camps of the Second World War, the system was carefully orchestrated to turn people against one another. Most of the prisoners could not resist this pressure, and no one should blame or judge them. But a few people understood that the strongest form of resistance was to refuse to focus on your own needs. It took extremely strong people to do that—truly unforgettable people—and they can teach us a lot about appreciation and survival. A recent book included an interview with an elderly woman who had spent several years in one of the camps. "What was it like?" she was asked. The woman chose her words carefully: "Well, at least in one way I'm grateful for having been there. Because it was a place where you could do a lot of good."

To make yourself an unforgettable person, recognize that where you are right now is a place where you can do a lot of good. It's also a place where a lot of good has been done for you. Then act accordingly—in other words, appreciatively—starting today.

Our second point: when you're thinking about what you can give and share, don't forget to include yourself as a possibility. We've focused on money as a means of appreciation in this chapter, but don't limit yourself to that. And especially don't limit yourself to money if you have a lot of it. If a businessperson has a net worth of $50 million, and he gives $10,000 to a charity, what did it cost him in terms of real appreciation? Was giving $10,000 a more appreciative act that giving an hour of his time? We've said that class is often a matter of doing what's difficult. That's especially true in terms of appreciation.

The flip side of this are people whose own circumstances are less than ideal. They'll say, "I have nothing to give. Don't bother me. Go ask a rich person." First of all, that's never true. Anyone can give a smile, a joke, a pat on the back, a word of encouragement, friendship, advice, and even love. Anyone can be rich in those qualities, and when you share them, you *feel* rich. When you say you have nothing, you're not *reflecting* a reality, you're *creating* a reality—and you're the one who has to live in it.

Here's another interesting thing about saying "I don't have

anything to give." With few exceptions, people who think that way don't suddenly change their attitude if their material circumstances change. If you won't give a dime when you have a dollar, there's an excellent chance you won't be any more appreciative even if you win the lottery tomorrow. Material situations can change, but attitudes are much less flexible. You can be an appreciative person right now simply by choosing to be one, and by behaving like one.

Point three: proactive, positive consciousness is an essential component of appreciation. If you act appreciatively only because you feel you have to, you forfeit the benefits of your action. If you make a donation to a university only to get your name on the front of a building, that is not an appreciative action no matter how much money you may have given.

Point four: class acts love to act appreciatively, and they look for opportunities to do so. Class and the absence of class are both habit-forming. One of the biggest obstacles to becoming an unforgettable person is simply the habit of not being one. We all know people who have been in the same job for thirty years or more—not because they like it, but just because it's what they've always done. The same is true with appreciation.

If you're not totally happy with what's happening with your career, your finances, or your life in general, ask yourself why. One of the things you can almost always change is the level of appreciation in your everyday experience. It's just a matter of deciding to make that change.

Start by asking, "What are the things in my life that are on automatic pilot? What do I do every day without even thinking about it?" Obviously, this doesn't refer to such things as brushing your teeth or taking out the garbage. What are your habitual behaviors that involve other people? Your habit might be going to work hard every single day from seven in the morning till eleven thirty at night. You tell yourself you'll see your kids maybe on the weekends. You're working for your kids so they won't have to work as hard as you do. But at the end of the day, you don't have a relationship with your children. You may be working *for* them, but maybe that's really an excuse. You've convinced yourself that you have to choose between one thing and another. Is there a more appreciative alternative? Is there a way you could give a little less to your work and a little more to your family? It might be a bit difficult at first. It might involve breaking some habits that you've gotten used to. But as we've said, class isn't easy, and it isn't supposed to be easy.

Let's look at another example. You're on an airplane flight. Out of the corner of your eye you glance at the person next to you, who is not impressive looking. If only it were Donald Trump, if only it were Jack Welch, if only it were Steven Spielberg! Why couldn't one of those people be on the plane with you? Then you'd find a way to start up a conversation. Even if you couldn't think of anything better than "Nice weather we're having," you'd find a way to take advantage of this lucky seating arrangement. Having a powerful and important person sitting next to you could help you in a lot of ways, and you would not let that chance pass by. But instead, as luck would have it, you're sitting next to a nobody.

Well, let me suggest a different way of looking at that situation. Instead of thinking, "This person can't help me," try thinking, "Maybe I can help this person." That's thinking appreciatively. That's thinking about giving instead of receiving. That's thinking about what can happen instead of what can't happen. Because how do you know what can't happen? Class acts don't focus on things they can't control—such as what another person can do. As a class act, you focus on what you can always control, which is what you can do at this exact moment.

Point five: appreciation always has a multiplying effect. As Dr. Robert Schuller has put it, "Anybody can count the seeds in an apple, but nobody can count the apples in a seed." Well, you may not be able to count the apples in a seed, but you can still get the idea that there can be a real lot of them. But you've got to plant the seed. Once you do, good things can start happening, and bad things can stop happening.

Here's a little story to illustrate what this means. A kind and trusting fellow named Ben lived in a small village that was flooding after forty straight days of rain. A rescue vehicle arrived on the scene, and the driver called to him, "Hurry, the entire village will soon be underwater. Get in!" Ben stood on his front porch, the water up to his ankles. "I'm staying right here. God will save me." Hours later, a boat arrived. The captain called for Ben to swim to the boat. Though the water had reached his waist, Ben refused. "I have faith that God will save me," he shouted. The boat motored off. By evening, the water had reached Ben's neck. A helicopter hovered overhead. A rescue line fell right in front of Ben. "Just grab the line," the pilot yelled. Ben waved the copter off: "I know God will save me!" The waters soon rose over Ben's mouth . . . his eyes . . . and finally his head. Ben drowned. In heaven, Ben requested a meeting with God. "I waited for you to save me," Ben cried. "What happened? Why didn't you save me?" "But, Ben," God replied, "who do you think sent the jeep, the boat, and the helicopter?!"

More than twenty years ago, the late Paul Newman decided he didn't have any money worries. He and a friend had an idea to start marketing a brand of spaghetti sauce. The marketing hook would be putting Paul's name and picture on the bottle. After several decades in the movies, however, Paul Newman didn't feel the need to have his face on a bottle any more than he felt the need for more money. But then he came up with an idea. The spaghetti sauce would be marketed, and there would be a picture of Paul Newman on the bottle, but all the money would go to charity.

This company was started in the most casual, unplanned way. But it did get publicity. Across the country, when people saw the drawing of Paul Newman on the bottle of spaghetti sauce, they bought that bottle instead of another one. Why? Because they thought it would taste better? No, they bought it because they had heard that the profits would go to charity. They had heard that this was an appreciative endeavor, and they wanted to participate in that appreciation. Believe it or not, that's the way things work.

Paul Newman's line of food products has generated almost $300 million in charitable contributions. It was created completely without the intention of getting any money at all for Newman and his partner. Was this the reason for its success? What do you think? Would people have bought the product if they thought it was going to buy another house or car for Paul Newman the famous actor? On the contrary, they bought the spaghetti sauce precisely because they knew that's what it wouldn't do. You can rest assured that this is an iron law in economics, as well as every other area of life. Appreciation has a multiplying effect. You can take that to the bank. You just can't deposit it in your own name!

Point six is in some ways the most powerful and the most interesting one. *Appreciation generates prosperity.* Giving to others translates into receiving for yourself. Appreciation is an investment, one of the best investments you can possibly make.

It could be interesting to try to document this with a lot of facts and figures. I'm not able to do that, but many people somehow instinctively know that giving is an investment. Sir John Templeton, one of the world's wealthiest people, said, "Appreciation has always been the best investment and the one that pays the greatest returns." How does this happen? Again, it's difficult to say. There's something mysterious about it. Mark Victor Hansen, cocreator of the *Chicken Soup for the Soul* books, has put it this way: giving puts the universe in your debt. Moreover, the return often comes in surprising ways and at unexpected times, and from unlikely sources. But somehow appreciation sets up an energy that pulls returns back to you like a magnetic field.

APPRECIATION IN THE WORKPLACE

The six points we've just discussed have applications in every area of your life, both business and personal. Now let's look at some suggestions that pertain specifically to the responsibilities of a class-act manager in the workplace.

As a leader and team builder, showing appreciation to your team can ensure a positive, productive, innovative organizational climate. Toward this end, a simple "Thank you" will encourage the actions and thinking that will make your organization successful. People who feel appreciated are more positive about themselves and their ability to contribute. People with positive self-esteem are potentially your best team members. These beliefs about team-member recognition are common among employers. Why, then, are they much less often carried out?

Time is one often-stated reason. Admittedly, team-member recognition does take time. Employers also start out with all of the best intentions when they seek to recognize team-member performance, but they often find their efforts turn into an opportunity for team-member complaining, jealousy, and dissatisfaction. After these experiences, many employers are hesitant to provide team-member recognition.

Beyond the time constraints, many managers don't know how to show appreciation effectively, so they have bad experiences when they try. They assume "one size fits all" when they provide team-member recognition. Leaders think much too narrowly about what team members will respond to in terms of appreciation. The suggestions that follow can help you expand your perspective and show your team members unforgettable appreciation.

Make it clear. Create goals for your team members and action plans that recognize the objectives, behaviors, and accomplishments you want to foster and reward in your organization.

Establish team-member recognition opportunities that emphasize and reinforce these sought-after qualities and behaviors. A two-copy written note is a good format. The team member keeps one copy, and the second is saved in the personnel file.

Fairness, clarity, and consistency are important. Your team needs to see that each person who makes the same or a similar contribution has an equal likelihood of receiving recognition for his or her efforts. I recommend that for regularly provided team-member recognition, organizations establish criteria for earning team-member recognition. Anyone who meets the criteria is then recognized. For example, if people are recognized for exceeding a production or sales expectation, anyone who exceeded the goal should be recognized. Glorifying only the highest performer will defeat or dissatisfy all of your other contributors, especially if the criteria are unclear or based on opinion.

Appreciation must be individualized. Consistent but also individual? Is this contradictory? Not really. Just make sure your recognition efforts don't become predictable entitlements that are passed around without any real excitement. This shouldn't be like handing out a gold watch—unless no one else has ever gotten a gold watch. "You did a nice job today" is a positive comment, but it lacks the power of "The report had a significant impact on the committee's decision. You did an excellent job of highlighting the key points and information we needed to weigh before deciding. Because of your work, we'll be able to cut six percent of the budget with no layoffs."

Offer appreciation immediately after the contribution you are recognizing. When a person performs positively, provide recognition right away. Chances are the team member is already feeling good about his or her performance. Your timely recognition of the team member will enhance the positive feelings. This helps everyone's confidence in the benefits of doing well in your organization.

Remember that appreciation is situational. People naturally have individual preferences about what they find rewarding and how appreciation is most effectively shown. One person may enjoy public recognition at a staff meeting; another prefers a private note in her personnel file. The best way to determine what a team member finds rewarding is just to ask.

Use all the available opportunities for appreciation. In many organizations, too much emphasis is on money as the preferred form of appreciation. While salary, bonuses, and benefits are critical within your team-member recognition-and-reward system, a class-act manager should have much more imagination.

Hopefully the ideas we've discussed in this chapter have convinced you that appreciation is in the best interests of everybody, both the giver and the receiver. In a literal way, appreciation equals prosperity.

But just in case you're not convinced, let's make one final point. Nothing is less appealing, and nothing is more comical, than an unappreciative person. Nothing looks more ridiculous than a miserly human being. Ebenezer Scrooge, in Charles Dickens's *Christmas Carol*, thinks he's important because he has a lot of money, but he's actually a pathetic individual because money is all he has.

In the past few years corporate America has been shocked by revelations of greed and financial fraud by executives of major corporations. These people had convinced themselves that they were masters of the universe. They had come to believe that the laws of giving and getting—and especially the laws of money—didn't pertain to them. They were wrong, because when it comes to appreciation, you will reap what you sow.

At the start of this chapter we referred to Adam Smith's statement that self-interest is the foundation of a well-functioning society. This is correct, provided that we recognize appreciation and generosity as the foundations of self-interest in the best sense. Our society as a whole may have a way to go in that regard, but as an individual you can activate those principles right away. And that's something you definitely ought to do.

Our next topic will be courage. The Greek philosopher Aristotle described courage as the foundation of all virtues. Courage is definitely one of the central elements of class. In chapter 15 we'll see why.

CHAPTER FIFTEEN

Courage, the Flip Side of Fear

Courage is a special human quality, and some would say it's becoming increasingly rare. The ancient Greeks believed courage to be the foundation of all other virtues, and there's a good chance the Greeks knew what they were talking about.

Consider this situation: A young, ambitious executive at a multinational company got a big promotion. There was only one condition. He had to move to Cairo, Egypt. He went home to his new wife and their baby and said, "Great news, we're moving to Cairo." His wife was stunned. She said, "You're moving alone. I'm going home to my mother."

This was a test of courage in that family. There was no viable compromise. If he relinquished his promotion, he would resent his wife for ruining his career; if she just went along with the move, she would hate him for ignoring her dreams for her baby and herself. What to do?

After some discussion, they might have been tempted to believe that maturity required them to deny their feelings and to sacrifice on behalf of each other. But instead, they went back to the fundamentals: Is it my career, or is it our career? Is it your baby, or is it our baby? Are we individuals, or do we operate as a team? What are our values? That marriage had to grow up by the equivalent of five years in about two weeks. They ended up going to Cairo, but their relationship had been transformed. She understood that his career was important to her. He recommitted to his values as a partner in the family. What matters is not what they ended up choosing, but how they made the choice. They took the courageous step to redefine, from the inside out, who they truly were.

What's the difference between a good general and a great general? Between an average parent and an outstanding one? Between a frightened child—and some are in their forties—and a mature adult? The difference is courage.

What makes some people crack under pressure—whether in warfare or business—while others seem to push themselves past their limits? Courage, or the lack thereof. Finally, why do some people challenge themselves to the limit—they even attempt the impossible—while others never get off the sofa? You should know the answer by now.

Courage is often understood to have two categories: physical and moral. Physical courage is the willingness to face serious risk to life or limb instead of fleeing from it. Moral courage is the firmness of spirit that faces danger or difficulty without flinching or retreating. The Civil War general William T. Sherman understood courage in almost mathematical terms. He said, "Courage is awareness of the true measure of danger, and the mental willingness to endure it." John Wayne put it more simply: "Courage is being scared to death and saddling up anyway."

Courage has been the mark of class acts throughout history, and that's not going to change anytime soon. Confronted with the same choices, some people stand up to accept the challenge while others shrink away.

What about you? Do you feel courageous? If so, please listen carefully to what follows. And if not, please listen even *more* carefully.

Of necessity, a discussion of courage must also be a discussion of fear. The Greek philosopher Aristotle made this point more than two thousand years ago.

WHAT IS IT, ANYWAY?

Mark Twain said, "Courage is resistance to and mastery of fear—not the absence of fear." Unforgettable people learn to master fear through experience and over time. But many men and women still live in fear throughout their lives. What is the difference, then, between people who master fear and those who are mastered by it?

To first control and then overcome fear, an unforgettable person must first learn what fear really is. The complicating factor is that fear exists in many different forms. In biomechanical terms, fear is a collection of hormonal responses released by the brain. Once these hormones disperse throughout the body, they begin to trigger defensive mechanisms such as raising adrenaline and cortisol levels, and increasing heart rate and respiration. This is the so-called fight-or-flight response. These symptoms are meant to stay active for only a few seconds or minutes, which is just enough time for a person to react to the object of his fear.

But what happens when that object of fear isn't real? What if it's simply a situation created by your imagination? For many people, the high levels of adrenaline and increased respiratory rates remain in the body for longer periods, adding more stress and consequently making the body experience "burnout" and total exhaustion.

Once you understand what your fears are as biological phenomena, the next step is to become consciously aware of their presence in a rational rather than an emotional way. You can do this in the form of a "thought experiment." When you start feeling anxious, take a moment in which you step back to say to yourself, "It's beginning. I'm becoming afraid." By acknowledging fear and keeping company with it, you will eventually learn how to master it.

Bear in mind that mastering fear does not mean destroying it. No one can ever completely destroy fear, nor is it necessary to do so. Fear will still be part of who you are whether you like it or not. But to help you reach an accommodation with this part of yourself, here are a few practical steps you can follow.

Get up and out. Many people have panic attacks early in the morning while they're still in bed. So get up and get moving. Get the morning paper, turn on the TV, and notice that life goes on around you. Get dressed and go outside. See that life and action are around you at all times. It puts your inner life into the correct perspective.

Exercise. Get moving enough to get the blood flowing. Do some sit-ups, push-ups, lift weights, and walk the dog a few blocks. Exercise replaces fear hormones in your body with neurochemicals that promote strength and power for longer periods.

Play some music. Turn on the iPod—or just whistle or sing! It's a great way to control your breathing and calm yourself down.

Live in the here and now. Certain words and phrases can help you detach from negative thoughts: "Relax" . . . "There's no problem" . . . "I'm in control." Saying this aloud will force you to concentrate on the tasks at hand and sway your mind from focusing on things in the future that may never occur.

Think positive. Reviewing a past success, particularly before a presentation or a meeting with your boss, is an excellent way to eradicate the butterflies. You're instantly reminded that you've achieved great things before, and there's no reason why you shouldn't achieve them again.

Food and fear. Eat something light and simple, such as toast with orange juice. It's hard to be afraid when you're eating, and it's especially hard to be in fear when the sugar and other nutrients from whatever you are eating enter your bloodstream.

Talk to yourself. Remind yourself of some basic facts about your life and your present situation. For example:

- *When you are in fear about things that you don't have or that you might lose—especially money, property, or employment—think about what you do have: a wonderful family, a loving dog, caring friends. The longer the list, the more your fear will evaporate.*

- *Always remind yourself that you are the master of your body and your mind. Never become a slave to your fears, especially when they begin to hurt others, such as your family or friends.*

- *Get plenty of rest. It's almost impossible to feel secure when you're exhausted or frightened.*

THE CHOICE IS YOURS

Faced with a charging lion or a maxed-out charge card, two people may both feel fear. But the courageous individual takes on the challenge, while the other does nothing. Courage matters—more than we think. Without courage, everything becomes fragile. Winston Churchill called courage "the first of human qualities, because it guarantees all the others." That's what we mean by the courage of our convictions. If we lack the courage to hold on to our beliefs in the moment of their testing, not just when they are in accord with those of others but also when they go against threatening opposition, then our beliefs mean nothing.

Courage doesn't always need to express itself in wars, arctic expeditions, or climbing mountains. Joining a fitness club can be an act of courage if you've gotten out of shape. In your career, you can display courage by fighting for an idea or a project you believe in, even if others don't agree with you. The point is, courage is an energy that manifests in our everyday lives by helping us control our fears. Even if fear is not completely overcome, it no longer holds dominion over our actions. We still feel fear, but how we react to that fear can demonstrate class to the world.

Of all the infinite varieties of fear, probably the most dangerous in the modern world is the fear of failure. Most of us are no longer faced with life-threatening adversaries. But we are faced with issues that can ruin our financial life, or our careers. Often that kind of fear boils down to a simple question: how does the possibility of success stack up against the risk of failure? Anyone who has ever wanted something badly enough in life has experienced the fear that comes with the possibility of failing. The greater the potential achievement, the greater the fear.

FEAR OF FAILURE

This is a common fear—and a really bad one! Fear of failure is closely related to fear of criticism and fear of rejection. Unforgettable people master their fear of failure, but others are incapacitated by it.

But in the largest sense, there is no failure; there is only feedback. Successful people look at mistakes as outcomes or results, not as failure. Unsuccessful people look at mistakes as permanent and personal. Buckminster Fuller wrote, "Whatever humans have learned had to be learned as a consequence only of trial and error experience. Humans have learned only through mistakes."

Most people self-limit themselves. Most people do not achieve a fraction of what they are capable of achieving because they are afraid to try and because they are afraid they will fail.

Take these steps to overcome your fear of failure and move yourself forward to getting the result you desire:

Take action. Bold, decisive action. Do something scary. Fear of failure immobilizes you. To overcome this fear, you must act.

When you act, act boldly. Action gives you the power to change the circumstances or the situation. You must overcome the inertia by doing something. Dr. Robert Schuller asks, "What would you do if you knew you could not fail?" What could you achieve? Be brave and just do it. If it doesn't work out the way you want, then do something else.

Persist. Unforgettable people just don't give up. They keep trying different approaches to achieving their outcomes until they finally get the results they want. Unsuccessful people try one thing that doesn't work and then give up. Often people give up when they are on the threshold of succeeding.

Don't take it personally. Failure is about behavior, outcomes, and results. Failure is not a personality characteristic. Although what you do may not give you the result you wanted, it doesn't mean you are a failure. Because you made a mistake doesn't mean that you are a failure.

Do things differently. If what you are doing isn't working, do something else. There is an old saying: "If you always do what you've always done, you'll always get what you always got." If you're not getting the results you want, then you must do something different. Most people stop doing anything at all, and this guarantees they won't be successful.

Don't be too hard on yourself. If nothing else, now you know what doesn't work. The perception of failure is a judgment of behavior. Look at failure as an event or a happening, not as a person. Treat failure as an opportunity to learn. What did you learn from the experience that will help you in the future? How can you use the experience to improve yourself or your situation? Ask yourself these questions:

- *What was the mistake?*
- *Why did it happen?*
- *How could it have been prevented?*
- *How can I do better next time?*

Look for possible opportunities that result from the experience. In *Think and Grow Rich*, Napoleon Hill wrote, "Every adversity, every failure and every heartache carries with it the seed of an equivalent or a greater benefit." Look for the opportunity and the benefit.

Fail forward fast. Tom Peters, coauthor of *In Search of Excellence* as well as author of many other extremely successful business books, says that in today's world companies must "fail forward fast." What he means is that the way we learn is by making mistakes. So if we want to learn at a faster pace, we must make mistakes at a faster pace. The key is that you must learn from the mistakes you make so you don't repeat them.

Fear, it should be clear, is the single biggest impediment to any sort of achievement. It's certainly a huge obstacle to making yourself an unforgettable person. In confronting fear with courage and commitment, one of the first steps is just recognizing fear. Some people never express courage because they don't even know they're afraid. They avoid challenges by such a wide berth that neither fear not courage ever have a chance to kick in. For others, just reading the word *fear* might cause a physical reaction. Fear can register on such a physical level that the simple thought of it is unpleasant. Your heart rate speeds up, your hands become moist, and all your senses are heightened. But in today's world, this usually isn't because someone is about to hit you with a battle-ax. It's because you're about to have a meeting with your boss. You're about to sign a mortgage agreement. You're trying to decide between two kinds of cars, or two investment plans. You're not afraid for your life. You're afraid of making a mistake. You're afraid of failure. Most often, you're just afraid of making a fool of yourself.

To help with this, remember that fear in the modern world is almost always a reaction to what's going on in your mind—because it's usually not going on anywhere else. As we discussed earlier, before your body can experience fear, your mind has to tell it to be afraid of something. Understanding that fear begins in the mind is a crucial step toward reacting courageously. Your brain may instinctively react with fear, but just by understanding that reaction, you can gain access to courage.

Fearful thoughts provoke physical symptoms and physical actions. Fearful thoughts cause sweaty palms, and fearful thoughts also cause missed sales and canceled projects.

At one time, gladiators may have dealt with their fears by building up their bodies. Today it's a matter of learning to control our minds. Some people are much better at this than others. Do you know somebody who always seems to be calm and collected? The kind of person that can't be rattled? Who's such a consistent model of courage, no matter what? Can it be that people like that don't have any fears at all?

The answer is—absolutely not. Everyone experiences fear, it's just that some people handle it better than others. People who achieve any level of success are able to master fear well enough to get things done. Class acts don't let fear stand in the way of making things happen. Just as an athlete learns to play through pain, a certain kind of businessperson works through fear to get a job done. How? Here are ideas you can try out for yourself.

First, remember what we said about fear being in the mind. In the contemporary world, fear is almost always a mind-created phenomenon. A class act understands this. A class act courageously attempts what others fear to do because a class act knows that the origin of fear is in our heads.

Second, remember that the most common form of fear in your working life is fear of failure. Even if it seems as if you're afraid of something else, fear of failure is almost always present in the workplace. Nobody likes to fail. It hurts the ego. It's not easy and it's not pleasant. But as we've seen throughout this book, class means doing what's difficult. Courage is the energy that lets you do that. Failure is a way of saying that you weren't good enough . . . not forever, just not this time. Just not yet.

If you look deeply enough into your fear, you will find that there's almost always nothing there. But fear tries to scare you into not looking closely. It's like the Wizard of Oz: "Pay no attention to the man behind the curtain." Fear scares you into not trying. Not trying deprives you of acquiring experience. Not acquiring experience means you are not moving forward. And if you don't move forward in any endeavor, how can you be successful? So look your fear in the eye, and you'll see that it can't really harm you.

This is what class acts have learned to do. Looking fear in the eye without blinking is the primary act of courage. In the seventeenth century, the British philosopher Francis Bacon said, "Nothing is terrible except fear itself." Three hundred years later President Franklin Roosevelt used almost those same words in the darkest hours of the Great Depression.

So if you feel the fear coming on before a big presentation or interview, call upon courageous thoughts. Remind yourself that you've been in more difficult situations before—and you're still here. You were probably made even stronger by the challenges you faced. In a year, or maybe a week, or perhaps even tomorrow, you'll feel the same way about what's happening today.

People often speak of conquering fears, but a much more effective strategy is to actually fall in love with them. Falling in love with fear means recognizing its symptoms and becoming aware of its presence, and devoting your conscious mind to it. Turn your fear into an experiment. When you start feeling nervous and anxious, tell yourself, "It's beginning. I'm becoming afraid." By acknowledging fear and keeping company with it, you will eventually learn how to master it.

Conquering fear in this sense does not mean destroying it. When you conquer something, you take control of it and become its master. No one can ever completely destroy fear, and why should you? It's a part of human nature whether we like it or not.

I'm sure it's clear by now that Fear is a precondition of courage, not its opposite. If we were looking for the real opposite to courage, there's a straightforward word for it: *dis*couragement. Like fear, it starts in the mind and directly affects what we do—or don't do.

In business, any endeavor is usually composed of many steps that are put together and ultimately lead to a goal. Building a company, for example, is an incremental undertaking. Along the way, you will likely get discouraged. Perhaps sales are not growing as fast as you would like; you hired some ineffective employees; one of your products had a defect; you had to issue a recall . . . the list is endless. You must keep in mind at all times that discouragement is part of the game. You will feel discouraged at times—which is when you must show the most courage.

Suppose you're a sales rep having a rough month. It looks as if you are going to miss your sales target and get chewed out by your boss. You start feeling down and become less productive. You figure you're done for. This is where the process begins; you have to realize that discouragement is sinking its claws into your mind. Recognize that you are starting to get discouraged.

Now you need to remind yourself—drill it into your head—that discouragement will get you nowhere. It will only help drag you down even more. So be quick and get it out of your system. Don't let it get a firm hold of you or you're toast. The faster you can get rid of it and get moving to reach your goals, the better. How can you do that? Good question. The answer is through *encouragement.*

This doesn't mean hiring the Dallas Cowboys cheerleaders. Encouragement can and must come from within. During your life, you've certainly achieved grand things. Maybe you won an award in your grade-school Olympics or got an A in a subject you liked. More recently maybe you were the top sales rep in your company for a time. Among other things, these achievements all required courage. More important, they are your achievements and nothing stops you from moving on to greater things. If you could stand up to the challenge and win back then, why not do the same today?

Tell yourself that you are capable of achieving great things. Tell yourself that you're smart. Tell yourself that you'll achieve your goals because you are willing to put in the necessary effort. Above all, tell yourself that you're a class act and an unforgettable person—in the past, in the present, and in the future.

Like many other emotions, both courage and fear are habit-forming. Have you ever been in a fear rut? This is particularly dangerous because you don't even see the fear that's behind it. You think you're in your comfort zone, but your real zone of comfort, the state of mind you really want to inhabit, is actually far away.

Even the phrase *comfort zone* has a nice lulling quality, doesn't it? It makes you think of sitting in a soft La-Z-Boy by a warm fireplace on a cold winter night. A relaxing and serene state no doubt. But be careful; taking a break once in a while is different from the comfort-zone rut, with the fear that is its true foundation.

The comfort zone includes all the familiar, everyday things you're accustomed to. Think of it as a circle in which you are at ease doing anything. There are no surprises here. If your boss walks in in the morning and asks you to run report ABC, as he does every morning, you won't even break a sweat. You know the drill. There is certainly nothing dangerous here—except the unspoken prospect of getting out of your comfort zone. And that's so scary that it never even enters your consciousness.

What if your boss came in one morning and told you to redesign a report from scratch? Suppose you also had to use a computer book you've never before seen. Suppose you had to have it done before noon. How would you feel then? The answer, of course, is uncomfortable. And maybe frightened, which is actually a good thing, because it brings you closer to the truth.

Now most people, when faced with a challenge that lies outside their comfort zone, will get nervous and panic: "I can't do this, I'll never get it done on time, I don't need this stress, why me, why not that other person in the next cubicle?"

But a class act meets challenges head-on. We learn by doing. Children don't learn to walk by watching others, they try to stand and fall hundreds of times before learning how to put one foot in front of the other in perfect balance. Doing things that are uncomfortable and new ultimately expands your comfort zone. It enables you to confront new tasks courageously—not without fear, but with fear under control.

If you do the thing you think you can't do, you'll feel your resilience, your hope, your dignity, and your courage grow stronger. Someday you'll face harder choices that might require even more courage. When those moments come and you choose well, your courage will be recognized by the people who matter most to you. When others see you choose to value courage more than fear, they will learn what courage looks like and they will only fear its absence.

So what's needed is action. But action does not spring from nothing. Suppose you wanted to start working out and get into top shape. To do so, you would have to start eating properly, go to the gym regularly, train with intensity, get enough sleep, and generally dedicate yourself to a given number of hours a week. Sounds like a lot of effort? Here's a secret: the hardest part is getting started. What makes the difference between a successful start and an unsuccessful one? Courage. You will need to build up your courage to the point where you can actually will something into existence.

Courage is essential for staying outside the trap of your comfort zone. Even if you are making great progress at the gym, it will take courage to stay away from alcohol, chocolate cake, or whatever else might bring you down.

Confidence and optimism are also essential. Courage is remaining optimistic through the most trying times, even when it looks pretty dark. Think about Nelson Mandela. Twenty-seven years of prison. I have to imagine he got a little discouraged, but from all accounts he never wavered in his confidence that South Africa would one day be a multiracial democracy. I am sure a few African National Congress people in prison with him said, "Nelson, you're making a hopeless mistake. This is ridiculous. Your optimism is misplaced here." In his deepest inner moments, I am sure Mandela had doubts. But as long as you can rekindle your optimism, you can find the courage to overcome any adversity.

Above all, have the courage to face this: in all areas of life, there are results and there are excuses. Results are not only what make you a success, they are what move society ever forward.

Excuses, on the other hand, keep you in the comfort zone, and they don't help anybody else out of it, either. Excuses invariably begin with the word *but,* which is why that's the most dangerous word in the English language. *But* allows us to stay in the comfort zone. It's the curtain behind which fear is hiding. Have the courage to pull that curtain back once and for all.

CHAPTER SIXTEEN

Money and Class

The mysterious relationship between those two words is why it's possible for a book such as this to be written in the first place. If class were simply a matter of getting rich, there would be no point in writing (or reading) anything on the subject that didn't deal with investments. If getting rich were the secret to making yourself unforgettable, the best way to spend your time would be by enrolling in business school.

The truth is, money can be as much an obstacle to class as it can be an entryway. That's the nature of money, which is "liquid." It takes the shape of the environment in which it exists. As an unforgettable person, you should have expectations beyond just acquiring a new car or a luxury home. These are fine to have, but "is that all there is?" Well, no, there's a lot more to do with money, and we'll be exploring some of it in this chapter.

Some people believe that money is everything, while others insist that money is nothing—and they're both right. Money is everything in the sense that currency can be transformed into virtually anything else simply by making a purchase. It can become a loaf of bread, a Ferrari, or a lifesaving surgery. But money is also nothing. It's just paper. Money has no inherent value; it's only valuable as a symbol of what it can buy.

Precious metals have been the basis for money's value for thousands of years, and it's unlikely that this foundation could suddenly be discredited. But there's no logical reason why that couldn't happen. Meanwhile, the value of paper money is constantly changing. Specifically, it's heading downward. The value of a dollar is now less than 5 percent of what it was when the Federal Reserve System came into being in 1913.

The confusing nature of money leads directly to our confused feelings about it. We should be rational about our money, and the science of economics does seem logical. Yet, it's built on some totally irrational assumptions. The value of money, for instance, was traditionally based on the underlying value of gold or silver. But why are gold and silver valuable? There's no logical reason. The foundation of the whole system is just an unspoken, arbitrary agreement that certain things are valuable and certain other things are not. Money has a psychological or even a spiritual foundation that's even more basic than its connections to reason and logic.

Interesting, right? But let's get serious. Exploring the history of money isn't going to pay your credit-card bill or your children's college tuition. And it certainly won't preserve your bank accounts in the case of severely negative changes in the economy—which is exactly what this book will help you do.

Money matters are always in flux. A never-ending cycle of rise and fall occurs in every area, from the price of gold to the price of milk. Sometimes changes in the cycle are sudden and dramatic. Booms occur, inevitably followed by crashes. But since a crash can be even more damaging than a boom is beneficial, it's vitally important to keep your personal finances from collapsing even during downturns in the larger economy.

Protect your job. Securing your financial future begins with protecting your present job—and protecting your job begins with *wanting* to protect it. Not all are fortunate enough to have work they love. Not all have work they can even enjoy. But if you can't stand your job, if it's all you can do to show up every day, you're not going to be effective in protecting it because—whether you admit it or not—you don't really *want* to protect it. You don't really want to be there in the first place.

Remember that you are probably not going to have this job forever. But make sure you have it as long as you want it. Make it as enjoyable as possible.

Ask yourself, am I only here because I'm afraid of not having somewhere else to go? If that's the case, *find* somewhere else. Find out where you really want to be and get there.

But if you truly have a reason to do your work besides just collecting a paycheck, then it's important to protect that work to the best of your ability. And it's not that difficult. Once again, a positive attitude is important—because plenty of people just aren't going to have that. So you can make yourself stand out just by putting a smile on your face. Or at least by not frowning.

Most companies have more than their share of negativity, complaining, and gossip. That's always been the case, and it's especially true in periods of economic contraction. So go in a different direction. Focus on the positive. Make a conscious decision to avoid the negative people. There may be a lot of them, but find the exceptions. If there are none, be the exception yourself. You can be totally in control of that possibility, so take advantage of that control.

But you *can't* control many things. In a corporate environment you can't determine the moods and whims of your supervisor or manager. The decisions made by the board of directors are most likely out of your hands. Again, *you* are what you can control—your work, your words, your actions, your attitudes.

The first step is determining what aspects of your job you are able to control, and what is beyond your influence. The behavior of your superior, the direction your company is taking, the rules and regulations the company imposes, these are all things you have absolutely no say in. What you can control is *you*—your behavior, your actions, your attitude, and—most important—your reaction to things you just have to live with.

Once you make the commitment to staying in your job because you want to stay in it, here are some specifics to keep in mind.

Know your company. What do you really know about the place where you work? Your answer should encompass much more than the company's product or service and profit or loss. Can you answer the following questions about your place of employment? If not, do something to change that situation as soon as possible.

- *What is the mission statement of your company? If there is none, what kind of statement could you make up?*
- *What obstacles do you face in trying to do your best work?*
- *What motivational support does the company provide? If there is no support, how can you motivate yourself?*
- *Do you feel empowered to make decisions and be creative? How does the company give you that feeling (or not give it).*
- *Are there any recent changes in the company that might have affected your motivation?*
- *Are your career goals and the goals of your company well aligned?*
- *How do other employees feel about the company?*
- *Are the company's internal image and external image consistent with one another? What about* your *internal and external image?*

Be confident. Think proactively about how you can make the greatest contribution to your company, then put those thoughts into action. Don't be afraid of making reasonable and well-intentioned mistakes. An employee who does nothing but "play defense" can't expect to score any points. It can be scary to see layoffs and cutbacks in your work environment, but it won't happen to you if you make yourself indispensable.

Concentrate on the "customer" and "the boss." Think of your boss as your customer and your customer as your boss—because that's what they really are. Your primary responsibility is serving your "customer's" needs. This doesn't mean groveling in front of your boss. Just recognize that a positive outcome for your supervisor will mean a positive outcome for you. Most managers don't like yes-men/women. Managers *do* like attention to their legitimate needs. Employees who fulfill those needs get rewarded. It's as simple as that.

Reach out. The word *networking* has been severely overused, but it is important to form positive relationships with as many people as possible in your work environment. In addition to your close colleagues, that means connecting with people from different departments and at all levels of responsibility. You never know who's going to get promoted and be in a position to help your career. Make sure that person isn't a stranger.

Blow your own horn. Without being heavy-handed about it, make sure your boss becomes aware of your accomplishments and contributions to the company. There is a fine line between kissing up to a manager and simply informing him/her of your contribution, so you've got to learn how to walk that line. It's a good idea to create an e-mail trail of your achievements. Some people will try to take credit for what you've done. The best way to prevent that is with solid evidence of what you did and when you did it.

Protecting your job requires attention, but it is not as hard as you might think. Just make sure you're convinced that you have a job worth protecting.

REDUCING DEBT

Debt is an extremely serious problem for a growing number of Americans. Let's look at some of the facts and figures. The average American family has $12,000 in credit-card debt and owns nine credit cards. A typical credit card with a $2,000 balance and a 19 percent interest rate will take you twelve years to pay off if you make the minimum monthly payments—and will cost you $4,000 total.

People in debt are faced with a nightmare of ever-increasing costs such as high credit balances and unfair interest rates, and they are finding it harder and harder to save. In addition, debt can take a terrible physical and emotional toll.

Debt reduction can be one of the most positive, rewarding, life-changing moves you'll ever make. Reduced debt can improve your health, leading to less stress, lowered blood pressure, and fewer headaches. A lower debt burden can also help maintain or rebuild your credit score, in case a loan is ever absolutely necessary. Fewer debts can also provide you with more freedom, which you could use to take time off work, pursue an education, or even to change careers.

Like hundreds of thousands of people in this country, you may feel you're hopelessly buried under a mountain of debt. But reducing it is very doable when it's approached in a systematic way. Follow the guidelines below to get started.

First, face the facts. It's not unusual for people in debt to be totally unaware of the reality of their financial situation. They live in a kind of denial that can make their lives complicated unless they do something about it. The first step is awareness of the problem. You face it squarely.

Here's how to go about that, step by step.

Make a list of all of the companies you owe money to (credit cards, car loans, store credit cards, student loans, etc.). Add up your credit debt and the cost of monthly payments. Now look at the total figure. You may be surprised at the amount. You may even be horrified. But at least you are aware, and that's the first step toward financial freedom and peace of mind.

Get rid of your nonessential credit cards. The fewer cards you have, the less temptation you have to spend. Cut the cards into pieces, then phone the card companies and inform them so that there is no chance of credit-card fraud. Do not acquire new cards.

Keep one card. This card is for emergency situations or travel, and it should be the card with the best rate and lowest annual fee. When choosing which card to keep, pay no attention to the introductory offer, as that does not last long enough to matter. Read the fine print on the monthly bill to determine which card is actually the least expensive. Prioritize your payments. High-interest and secured debts should be paid first. These include mortgage and car payments. With all debts, exceed the minimum monthly payment whenever possible. By doing so, you can reduce the debt faster and save money by avoiding the accrued interest.

Consolidate your debts to the greatest possible extent. Transfer all of your credit card balances to the card with the lowest interest rate. Doing this may seem like a hassle, but if you can reduce interest rates by even a fraction, that can save you a surprisingly large amount of money.

As your debt reduction efforts start to work, use the money you've saved to further pay down your obligations. Being totally debt free is the ultimate goal. It's a high-priority mission with you as both the cause and the beneficiary. You have to be willing to go to any lengths to raise enough money to be free of debt as quickly as possible. And permanently.

"PUSH BACK FROM THE TABLE"

When things are going great in the economy, it's easy to think that this situation will continue forever. Once the situation changes, it's also tempting to believe it will never recover. Nobody knows what the financial future holds, and in a certain sense it doesn't matter. The real issue is, whatever happens, will you have the strength and information to deal with it in the best possible way?

People respond in many different ways to financial challenges. Many slip into a kind of denial, refusing to accept that they have to adapt—or more specifically, that they have to cut back.

The art to surviving hard times lies in pushing back from the table without starving yourself to death. You'll want to have a realistic assessment of your situation without lapsing into a mentality of scarcity and deprivation.

Start by examining your relationship to money. What do you hope money will bring you? What do you fear you'll lose if money is not as plentiful as it was in the past? Then get more specific. How aware are you of the nonnegotiable costs of maintaining your lifestyle? The utility bills? The car payments? The rent or mortgage? Many people have a surprisingly vague grasp of what their financial responsibilities actually are. During difficult economic times, however, no one, not even the wealthy, can afford to be vague about his or her finances. Things are changing too quickly for that, and at least in the short term, they're probably not changing for the better.

Once you have a clear view of what your "nut" is, you can move on from the financial responsibilities that you can't change to those that you can control. Simply put, these are the areas in which you can cut back—and it won't be nearly as painful as you might think. There's a good chance you'll feel more liberated than constrained. Often we start out thinking of something as a luxury, and before long it seems like a necessity. But that's only because we've fallen into the trap of mistaking luxuries for entitlements.

This new awareness is more than just a step toward saving money. It's another opportunity to put yourself in control, which will help combat any feeling of powerlessness and victimization that an economic downturn can bring on. Along with a frank, realistic look at your spending, you'll also need commitment and willingness to change. Market conditions in housing, stocks, and other investments may bring complications, so prepare yourself to take them on rather than hide from them. The major requirements are common sense, awareness, and the decision to take positive action.

To get through a downturn with as little discomfort as possible, a typical family will definitely need to reduce spending, and sometimes dramatically so. The first place to look is to high-cost items that are not really matters of life and death. Expensive vacations, new cars, sports events—these are discretionary rather than necessary. You can cut them out a lot easier than you can eliminate medical prescriptions or the heating bill.

Here are a few ways to reduce your spending. There are many, many more. Brainstorm with your friends and family members and you'll come up with plenty of ideas.

Internet, cable, and phone services. If you take the time to closely examine the bills for these services, you will discover that you are probably paying for more services than you use. Stop paying for what you don't use.

High-speed Internet service has become a necessity in today's world. It's an essential utility like electricity or gas. But there are significant variations in price from one provider to another, and you may not need all the bells and whistles that some companies try to sell. If you can sign on to the Web and access your e-mail, you've probably got everything you need.

If you ever have a problem with your service—and most people do sooner or later—don't hesitate to bring it to the attention of your provider. Often they will discount your bill, especially if they think you're angry enough to discontinue the service.

If you use your cell phone a great deal, it probably makes sense to cancel your landline account. Keep in mind, too, that the Skype Internet phone service is virtually free for domestic calls, and only about $10 a month for worldwide service.

Food. For years shoppers have chosen to purchase nationally advertised name products over the store brands. That may have been a wise decision at one time, but no longer. Store-brand products are the same quality as brand-name products—in fact, they may come from the same wholesale source—and they typically cost 20 to 50 percent less. Look for meat, poultry, and fish that are on sale. The savings are significant, especially when you buy in bulk and use your freezer.

Gasoline. There is no reason to use anything other than regular gasoline unless you own a Ferrari—and if you do own a Ferrari, now might be a good time to sell!

Prescription drugs. Always check with your doctor or pharmacist to see if the medication you are being prescribed can be had in the generic form. There is virtually no difference in quality between the brand name and the generic, and the price difference can be significant.

Home heating. Dial the thermostat a single degree lower for eight hours a day and you'll save 5 percent on your winter heating bill.

Subscriptions. If you are comfortable reading at your computer, think about canceling your newspaper and magazine subscriptions and read them online. You may not even have a choice.

Many publications are simply discontinuing their hard copies and going completely electronic.

Research shows that 60 percent of all Americans are worried about running out of money. Instead of worrying, do something about it. Take action. Instead of indulging, save, reduce, and conserve. Regardless of how much you actually save, your efforts alone will allow you to let go of the feelings of powerlessness and victimization that a downturn often causes.

STAY CALM, STAY POSITIVE

During periods of financial challenge, people commonly feel overwhelmed or even panicked. It's an understandable reaction, but unfortunately that response can only make things worse. Until the external situation improves, the best and most effective way to ride out the storm is to stay calm and positive. And if you're thinking, "Easier said than done," well, let's see how to do it.

When thinking about the most effective ways to stay calm, it's useful to think in terms of *internal* and *external* life. The first deals with what goes on in your head, your thinking, emotions, and attitudes. External life is about what you actually do: your actions, reactions, and other behavior.

INTERNAL LIFE

Start being kind to yourself. Nobody's perfect. Stop demanding perfection from yourself and everyone you know. Your best on any given day is enough. If you lower your expectations and try to accept or even celebrate imperfection, you will experience so much less tension and your life and job will go way more smoothly.

Put away the magnifying glass. Making mountains out of

molehills is only going to give you a gigantic headache. Try to put things in their proper perspective. When faced with a difficult situation or dilemma, ask yourself, "How important is this really?" The bigger you make it, the harder it will be to deal with.

Procrastination kills. We all tend to leave things until the last minute. This is particularly true for people with busy, active lives. But the amount of stress and tension procrastination causes is off the charts. Managing your time and learning to do work in increments will make a world of difference.

EXTERNAL LIFE

Breathe deep. Most people do not breathe properly. They take shallow breaths or even unconsciously hold their breath for periods of time. In doing so, they are robbing themselves of relaxation and good health. Pay attention to your breathing. A few times a day, stop whatever you're doing and breathe deeply. Fill your lungs and hold it for a moment. Now exhale through your nose. The affect is calming and should allow you to work more effectively.

Play well with others. For many people the most unnerving part of daily existence is interacting with other human beings. The practice of "live and let live" is strongly recommended. The understanding that in the short term there is little—or perhaps absolutely nothing—that you can do to change anyone else is a key to peaceful coexistence. The best you can do is to accept your fellows and to communicate as clearly as possible with them, always remembering that no one can read minds.

Work it out by working out. It is amazing how much physical exercise can contribute to a feeling of calm. You've probably heard of endorphins, the chemicals released in the brain during exercise that promote feelings of well-being. Endorphins are real, as is the self-esteem that comes from taking care of oneself. It doesn't have to be a two-hour workout or a marathon handball contest. A simple jog around the block can rid you of unwanted stress and anger.

Sleep tight. Another basic resource of calm is restful sleep. This seems obvious, but the importance of sleep is often ignored by people under stress. Yet nothing insures clear thinking and restored energy like a good night's sleep. And nothing is more ruinous to one's health or effectiveness on the job than poor sleep. Alcohol and caffeine should not be consumed shortly before bed. Reading a comforting book or taking a warm bath helps to guarantee a good night's sleep. In addition, getting into the habit of a good night's sleep usually removes the necessity for naps during the day, and that time can be devoted to work.

As with staying calm, the segment on staying positive is divided into internal life and external life.

INTERNAL LIFE

Check your perceptions. Many negative thoughts are based on an incorrect perception of the situation. People tend to imagine and buy into a worst-case scenario. That's why it's important to clearly and rationally examine the facts of your situation. Often if you remove the emotion from the perspective, the picture looks decidedly more realistic and optimistic.

Worst-case scenario. You can also use the worst-case scenario to your advantage. Allow yourself to imagine the absolute worst possible outcome for whatever situation you're dealing with. Really look at it. Face the fear. Feel how it would feel. Once you return to reality, you have a sense of having faced the worst, and of having survived it. This experience will make it that much easier to cope with whatever you wind up dealing with.

Paint positive pictures. Just as you used your imagination to conjure up images of your worst-case scenario, you can do the same to achieve the opposite. Think of an upcoming situation. Imagine how things would be ideally. See yourself in the vision. Watch everything go perfectly. Add all the details you possibly can to the picture. Make it as real as possible. Do this whenever you want. A particularly good time is right before bed.

EXTERNAL LIFE

Watch what you say. Your brain hears and believes the messages you send it. Whatever you say or think, no matter how ridiculous or unrealistic, may be taken as truth by your subconscious. Therefore, it's a good idea to pay attention to your thoughts and words, and when you become aware of negative messages, change them to positive ones. This takes practice, but you can actually reboot your thinking, which in turn impacts your entire life.

Don't ignore your feelings. When you have negative feelings and you stuff or ignore them, they continue to live inside you, festering and snowballing. These feelings still have emotional weight, and you have to drag them around with you like luggage. The best way to process or let go of these feelings is simply to find someone to talk to about them—someone you trust, a friend, colleague, or relative. Even a therapist. Unburden yourself. Holding on to negative feelings will do you no good. It certainly won't make you any money.

INVEST IN YOURSELF

If there's one thing wealthy, successful businesspeople agree on, it's that learning doesn't stop after college. They know they got where they are because of their continuing commitment to improving and deepening their knowledge.

Learning is always key to career advancement, but especially during a time of economic contraction. Companies are downsizing, jobs are lost, and employers are taking a harder look at their employees to see if they merit being kept on the payroll.

This is a time of risk, of keen competition, when your value to the company needs to be as great as possible. The best way to remove the risk and to increase your value is to invest in yourself. This means learning new skills, developing better contacts, and expanding your knowledge. To accomplish this you must become proactive. Don't wait for opportunity to find you. You've got to find opportunity.

START WITH YOUR OWN COMPANY

Your company undoubtedly has a human resources department. Familiarize yourself with its policies. Some companies offer professional development plans and may even finance them. This would be ideal as education costs can be quite expensive.

CONTINUING EDUCATION

You might want to make a potentially win/win proposal to your manager. Request that the company pay for your further education. You will have to make a bulletproof case as to how your new knowledge will benefit the company, but this is not especially difficult to do. It helps that any expense to your company will most likely be a tax deduction. Just check up on this before you make your proposal.

You may not have to take time off from work to advance your education. Much of this can be done online. There will still be some expense, but you can make the case to your company that the advantages of more education can now be had at significantly less expense than ever before.

NETWORKING

There are lots of ways to broaden your outreach for your benefit and for the good of your company.

- *Business networking events.* Lots of high-end industry conferences and seminars are available, but you may learn just as much at the smaller networking events in your area. They are not hard to find.

- *Local chamber-of-commerce events.* These are great places to make business contacts and find new leads for your company. They usually doesn't cost anything.

- *Special-interest venues.* Focused gatherings such as venture-capital forums are more common than you think, and often in your own city.

- *Business luncheons.* Your company might have knowledge of informal business luncheons, which are becoming quite common. All you have to do is ask. This is the kind of thing that would keep you away from the office for only a couple of hours.

PERSONAL SELF-IMPROVEMENT

The most economical method of self-improvement is the lost art of reading. It can be done on your own time, it's extremely cost-effective, and you don't even have to plug a book into the wall!

So take a trip to your local library or bookstore. Give yourself some time to browse. You'll be surprised at how much has been written about your particular areas of interest. Make a commitment to read at least one book per month. It's a good idea to use the *New York Times'* bestseller list as a resource for selection of reading material. Consult it each week in the Sunday book review. There's a good chance you'll be surprised by the number of books that relate to your specific interests.

Investment in yourself is absolutely the best investment you can make for securing your future. Yes, it takes some of your free time and energy, and you will have to prioritize. But you'll meet new people, you'll make new friends, and you'll learn something. It's an excellent bargain.

GET HELP

There are many sources of assistance for preventing financial problems, as well as for dealing with them if and when they do occur. Friends and family members are the obvious first choice, but you may not feel comfortable disclosing your financial difficulties to those closest to you. Why this should be the case is an interesting question, but we don't have to answer it here. Instead, let's look instead at outside resources for dealing with money-related issues.

FINANCIAL PLANNERS

Personal financial planners are professionals who advise couples or individuals on managing their money. Typically this involves estate planning, tax planning, and sometimes dealing with debt. But for the most part, financial planners are not crisis managers, and they're also frequently oriented toward more affluent clients. Quite often they will not only evaluate a person's financial condition, but also attempt to sell investments to a client. There is nothing wrong or unethical about this, but it may not meet the needs of a substantial part of the population. Also, meeting with a financial planner can be quite expensive, usually between $150 and $300 per hour.

COACHING

For many people, affiliating with a personal financial coach is an attractive option. Coaches' clients are not usually limited to individuals in upper income brackets, and coaches do not generally try to market investment instruments. However, certification for personal financial coaches may not be as well organized or as rigorous as certification for financial planners. For that reason, it's important to clearly define your needs and expectations, and to look carefully at the qualifications of the coach you hire to fulfill them.

The qualities required for good coaching are different from those needed by other financial professionals. Here are some of the skills you should look for in a coach. You can and should recognize them before the subject of money even comes up.

Listening. In coaching, listening is actually more important than talking. By being listened to, people can be helped to overcome their fears, be offered complete objectivity, and be given undivided attention and unparalleled support. This leads to the intuitive questioning that allows clients to explore for themselves what is going on. You need to feel your coach is an excellent listener before entering into any kind of ongoing arrangement. If the listening capability isn't there, nothing else can make up for it.

Communication skills. Coaching is a two-way process. While listening is crucial, so is being able to interpret and reflect back, in ways that remove barriers, preconceptions, bias, and negativity. Communicating well enables trust and meaningful understanding on both sides.

Coaches are able to communicate feeling and meaning, as well as content—there is a huge difference. Communicating with no personal agenda, and without judging or influencing, is essential, especially when dealing with people's anxieties, hopes, and dreams.

Good coaching uses communication not to give the client the answers, but to help the clients find their answers for themselves.

Rapport-building. A coach's ability to build rapport with people is vital. Normally such an ability stems from a desire to help people, which all coaches tend to possess. Rapport-building is made far easier in coaching compared to other services because the coach's only focus is the client. When a coach supports a person in this way, it quite naturally accelerates rapport-building.

Motivating and inspiring. Coaches motivate and inspire people. The ability to do this lies within us all. It is born of a desire to help and support. People who feel ready to help others are normally able to motivate and inspire. When people receive attention and investment from a coach toward their well-being and development, this is motivational and inspirational.

GIVING IT ALL AWAY. OR AT LEAST SOME OF IT

If you've learned one thing from this chapter, it should be that money is not an end in itself. It's only significant because of what it can do, and you are the one who makes that determination. The main goal of some people for their money is to provide an estate for their children. "I don't want them to have to do what I went through" is how it's usually put. Other people are concerned that their estates not fall into the hands of the government's inheritance tax. They're less concerned with what they can do with their money than what somebody else might do with it if given the chance. A third group sees things completely differently.

Some wealthy people want their heirs to inherit less than the full amount of the estate. This is based on the belief that human nature does not benefit from unearned wealth: "You need to make money the old-fashioned way. You need to earn it."

The best-known proponent of this belief is Warren Buffett, the icon of stock-market investing and one of the world's wealthiest people. Buffett has long been an advocate of low taxation, with one important exception. He would support an inheritance tax of 100 percent. That way everyone starts life on a level playing field, no matter what the person's parents and grandparents might have done. In theory, this would ensure that everyone tries harder and the entire society benefits.

Actually, there have been varying reports of how far Warren Buffett wants to go with this. He may not advocate the complete elimination of inheritance, but he definitely wants to limit it. He has often said that wealthy parents should leave their children with enough money to have what they want, but not enough so they do nothing at all. He has also pledged a $31 billion legacy to the Bill and Melinda Gates Foundation—a tidy sum that will be going outside his family forever. As a result, Warren Buffett has opened a fundamental debate about the concept of a financial legacy. Is it better to limit what you pass on and not spoil your heirs, or to let them inherit the wealth and build on it? Whatever you choose to do with your estate, building one incorporates many of the same techniques as saving for a second home or your children's education.

First, where do you ultimately want to be in financial terms? Setting a financial goal is no different from choosing a travel destination. You're trying to get somewhere with your money. You're trying to reach a certain goal—and knowing your goal means everything in money management. If you don't know where you want to be, you won't know how to get there. And you won't know how to avoid or minimize the risks along the way. You may not even recognize the risks at all.

Second, how much time do you have to get where you want to be? The time you have to reach your financial destination will determine the level of urgency you feel. Again, it's like planning a trip. Once you see how far you have to go, you may be comfortable with the time you have to get there, or you may need to give yourself more time, or you may need to adjust your goal to meet your deadline.

Time is a huge factor in investing. The relationship between your time and your objective will always play a role in your planning. If you have five hours to travel five hundred miles, you'll plan your trip differently than if you have five hours to travel only a tenth of that distance. It's the same with money. You have to know how far you need to go and in what frame. That's the only way to create an intelligent plan for getting there.

Question number three: Where are you now in your financial life? How much money can you put toward your goal at this moment? What's your starting point? The answer to this comes in two parts: your net worth, which is the total value of everything you own, minus the debts you have to repay; and your monthly cash flow, which shows your monthly income and spending patterns. It's a snapshot of how money flows into and out of your life. When this information is clear in your mind, you can start making informed decisions. If you want to create a passive income legacy of $200,000, for example, you'll be able to see how much money you can designate toward this goal right now. You might have $25,000 in a retirement plan and $15,000 in a savings account. You don't want to touch your retirement account, but perhaps you can move some money from your savings into a vehicle that will benefit your heirs.

Fourth and last, what financial vehicles will let you meet your goals in the time available? When you plan a trip, you need to know how far you have to travel and how long you have to get there. Once you have that information, choosing the vehicle and the route should be obvious. Investment and estate-planning decisions can be clear, too. You just have to know your legacy goals and be familiar with the vehicles that can get you there.

There's more to say about legacy planning that goes beyond the scope of this book, and there's much more to say about money and class. Lest you become overwhelmed, chapter 17 will offer some tools for living comfortably as a class act—not just comfortably in your country estate, but in your own skin.

CHAPTER SEVENTEEN

Don't Worry, Be Classy

So much has been written about goal setting over the years. There's a section on the topic in virtually every book dealing with personal development. But there's a reason for this. People realize the importance of goals and they want to do it correctly. So with the understanding that our ultimate goal is to become a class act and an unforgettable person, let's look at what successful goal setting—and goal achievement—involves.

Setting a personal or professional goal is a rewarding accomplishment in itself. However, goals are not without their dangers. If you shirk other responsibilities or cut corners simply to meet the objective you've set for yourself, the costs can be bigger than the payoff.

Moreover, from the beginning, goals must be set neither too high or too low. And the time frame for their achievement needs to be challenging but attainable.

From the beginning, see the end. Can you envision an oak tree when you hold an acorn in your hand? It's not logical, but you know it can happen. Can you imagine a multimillion-dollar company when you write an idea on the back of a napkin? That can happen, too—maybe—but it's up to you. Most people's back-of-the-napkin plans come to nothing. But not every acorn becomes a tree, either.

Although some books use the terms almost interchangeably, a goal is not the same thing as a dream. Goals must be realistically attainable, not just theoretically possible. Dreams have their place, certainly. The power of a vision, no matter how far-fetched, can change your life. But don't build your day around winning the U.S. Open tennis tournament unless somebody besides yourself has told you that's a good idea. Fantasy is fun, but it's not reality.

Envisioning a realistic outcome—mentally seeing yourself reach your goal in the real world we live in—is a crucial first step in goal setting. An "inner movie" of you reaching your goal is extremely valuable. The movie can even be a comedy. But it can't be a cartoon!

Make a list of the practical steps involved. Such a list will be another step in bringing you down from the clouds and into the real world. It will clarify what's really necessary in getting started and eliminate what's merely fluff.

If you want a new job or a different career, you'll need to update your résumé—that's the first step on your list. Others might include researching the job market and finding websites on which to post your new résumé. As you continue your list—including target dates for accomplishing each item—be aware that simply deciding that you want a new job isn't a clear enough goal. When you set a goal, it needs to be defined by the destination, not the departure. Writing "in six months I want to have a new job" is much too vague. You could have a new job that's even worse than the present one. In that case, has the goal been attained? Writing a good list can help you focus on *exactly* what you want, which is a key step toward getting it.

Identify potential obstacles and plan around them. Barriers on the path to achieving your goals come in all shapes and sizes. They're much less of a threat, however, when you've seen them ahead of time. This doesn't mean you should focus on every single thing that could possibly go wrong. There will always be surprises, and some setbacks are unavoidable. But you want to be prudent enough so that encountering a problem doesn't cause your goal to suddenly collapse.

For example, unexpected financial obligations can be a setback if your goal is to save enough money for a home—so, expect the unexpected. Create a special savings account as an emergency fund. Make a deposit into that account every month. It can be a small deposit, but it will prove significant if and when you need it.

Track your progress. Keep on track to your goals with the help of a journal. This can be a computer file or a hard copy, but it should be updated frequently—several times each week at least. The journal can also be a place to add notes, make alterations to your goal, and to see what you've accomplished over time. In addition, your journal can inspire you to keep on course if you start to drift off, and it can give encouragement by documenting how far you've come.

Goal setting and goal achievement are fundamental to making yourself an unforgettable person. And they're ongoing. You should always be on the lookout for new worthwhile goals, even before you've achieved your current ones. The steps below will help you to identify new opportunities and build them into your plans.

Recognize the ongoing need for new opportunities. Most people, in looking back over their lives, can see moments of opportunity that they simply failed to see. That's okay. It happens to everybody. But it's not something that you want to happen again. Can you be certain that, if an opportunity presented itself today, you would recognize it? Many people spend the majority of their time on automatic pilot. Their minds aren't open to opportunities; they're not actively alert to them. Yet good luck does indeed favor those who are prepared to receive it.

The first step toward seeing new opportunities is deciding that, whether in your career or your personal life, things could be even better than they are if you found something new. It takes some class to admit this. Honesty is required to admit, if only to yourself, that the life you've worked so hard to attain can still benefit from improvements, and that seeing new opportunities is the means toward the end.

Draw inspiration from others. Educate yourself about the circumstances that have led other men and women to discover opportunities. Behind every major success—whether it's that of Isaac Newton or Bill Gates—there is a story of hard work, good luck, and a gift for seeing what other people missed and taking advantage of it.

Go beyond your comfort zone. Fresh opportunities are nearly impossible to spot when you stay where you've always been. Fear, avoidance, or just plain inertia are the enemies of opportunity. Personally and professionally, almost all of us have a comfort zone that insulates us from recognizing opportunity when it arises. It's almost astonishing that we can so easily conform to the monotony of a job, find comfort in it, and even feel fretful at the possibility of change—despite that change could be exactly what's in our best interests.

But that's what a comfort zone is. Ultimately, it's destructive and profoundly limiting. But it's so comfortable! Whatever your comfort zone might be, to recognize opportunities and make changes to any aspect of your life, you will have to first acknowledge that you're in that zone and take the uncomfortable steps to get out of it.

Strip away your preconceived ideas. If an opportunity presents itself that is outside your norm, don't succumb to the temptation not to pursue it just because "it probably won't work." Or because it's too expensive. Or because it's too risky, or too fraught with potential disappointment. The last step in recognizing opportunities is to set aside these reflexive biases. Learn to see beyond knee-jerk negativity and see an opportunity for what it is. It may work and it may not. But it's an opportunity to be considered, not just ignored or avoided.

For example, you may not think your current job is ideal for you, but with the current state of the economy you may tell yourself you should be grateful to have a job at all. There's nothing overtly wrong with this viewpoint. It makes perfect sense. But it shouldn't obscure your judgment about other opportunities and cause you to reject them out of hand the moment they arise. They certainly shouldn't be rejected simply because the idea of leaving your job is too threatening. Instead of assuming that your current employment is your lifeboat during the economic crisis, and that anything else is too dangerous to consider, why not consider that new opportunities are created even during troubled times—and that one of them might be right for you?

True, there's a certain amount of risk in this. But worthwhile goals and reasonable risk are two sides of the same coin. Setting goals in life speaks to everyone because we all have new things we'd like to do, make, or be. However, getting started on the road to something new can be difficult. Many of us tend to focus on failure and the unknown. It can be a little intimidating: we're unsure of ourselves around the unknown and the possibility of failure. But that's also why we're drawn to goals in the first place. There's a natural desire to launch into the unknown, to head into unfamiliar territory and find out what awaits beyond the horizon.

Taking risks is tough but necessary. As an unforgettable person you will do many things in your lifetime, but when you look back on them, you will see that nothing worth having was simply handed to you. That involves risk—which can be assessed and managed by the following steps.

See the payoff through the risk. Recognize risk when you see it, but before you take any action, have some fun with the risk. Imagine what wild success would look like if you took the risk and succeeded. Visualize this in great detail. What would it feel like, taste like, and smell like? Every bit of additional detail will help. Painting this exciting picture will clarify why you might want to try something new, even with its risky possibilities. Knowing your "why" will help when the going gets rough, as it well might.

In addition, having fun with risk lets you focus on the positives rather than the negative possibilities. Starting something new can be scary, but you need to pay attention to what you stand to gain, not "what's the worst than can happen?"

Finally, mentally connecting with the ultimate goal ensures you're heading in the right direction and helps you take risks accordingly. You may be trying your hand at cooking dinner for the first time, and you're dreaming of creating a gourmet dinner. But then you find yourself buying hot dogs in the grocery store. Yes, you're headed toward "success"—you're going to make "dinner"—but you are not going to achieve the goal that's in your heart. If you take the risk, you might eventually fail. But if you don't take the risk, you've failed already.

Acknowledge the hard parts. You've decided you're willing to take a risk, but you haven't yet taken action. Why is that? Think through the risk you're thinking of taking and identify the opposition. Your mind will drift to the areas you see as being resistant on the path to your goal. At first this will look murky. That's because you haven't taken the time to find out what's between you and your goal. To take risks, you need to get specific about the things you'll need to overcome. They may be physical obstacles (lack of funds, or not having the right equipment) or intangibles, such as fear of the unknown or lack of time to start something new.

Suppose you want to learn to play a musical instrument. Thinking through why you haven't learned yet, you might realize you don't own a guitar, don't know anything about one, don't have money for one, and don't know how to go about learning. That's a lot of difficulty, but at least now you're clear on what you need to do. From there, your creativity and willpower will start to solve the problems. Your unconscious mind can solve many problems. What your unconscious mind *can't* do is penetrate the murky mass of fear between you and your goal. So bring this into the light of day. Does one of your friends have a guitar in a closet collecting dust? What about a tuba?

Get started! Mark Twain said, "The secret to getting ahead is getting started." The biggest obstacle to change is internal resistance. It's easy to get caught up in analysis paralysis and spend your days sketching out your perfect route to achieving your goals. However, at some point you simply need to start. This is the hardest part, and unfortunately there aren't any secret tips or tricks, just your willpower and the doing. That's why, as soon as you're clear on your goal and are ready to take risks, you should get started—even if it's a rocky start. An imperfect start is always better than a perfect daydream, and much better than a good excuse.

Enjoy the ride! Once you've embraced the risks and started down the road to your goal, enjoy the ride. Success doesn't necessarily come quickly, but by simply starting down the road, you're closer to your dream than you've ever been before. Anything worth doing is going to come with a price—it's an essential part of taking risks. Be proud of yourself just for starting.

It can be easy to get discouraged, so keep positive. Enlist friends to keep you accountable, and talk with them about your goal whenever you hang out. Talk about your goal with everyone you know: people at work, the checkout girl at the grocery store, etc. You'll be reminded of your goal each time others ask how your goal is coming along. Don't forget to ask them what their goals are. You'll be surprised at how few people actually have clearly defined goals! That will provide motivation in its own right. You're one of the few people you know trying to achieve something difficult.

It's tough to get started on something new, but that's what makes it worth doing. Taking risks lets you discover new things about the world and about yourself. It brings new pleasures and accomplishments into your life. It can expand your horizons and open the world to you. None of those is going to happen to you if you're just sitting on the couch and not being open to taking risks. Strap on your pith helmet and get in the game of life. Look past the risk, identify the obstacles you need to overcome, then get started. Take the time to enjoy the ride and start thinking of what you'll do next. Because if you stick with it, you can and will achieve a well-thought-out and carefully planned goal.

The only variable is time, and within time the only variable is constant change and transformation. Change can modify, alter, amend, even shatter, but it always transforms. Few of us like it and even fewer thrive on it. In the past, the lives of many people didn't change much over the years. They were born on the same farm where they would later die. But that's not the way we live now, and this involves change at a deeper level than just the introduction of a new model iPhone.

Some common examples of change include:

- *Moving away from a place you've called home.*
- *Changing careers.*

- *Ending a meaningful relationship.*

- *Dealing with physical changes and challenges—everything from weight gain or hair loss to something more serious.*

Accept the change as an ongoing reality. In any important life process, acceptance is typically the last phase, not the first. But acceptance is always fundamental when confronting change because "you can't fight city hall." Defiance or denial only delays the inevitable.

So how does an unforgettable person go about reaching acceptance? First, avoid trying to deny or even soften the personal impact of change by carrying with you too many elements from the status quo you are now leaving. At the same time, you should maintain at least some of your well-established routines and relationships. Make an effort to keep seeing people whom you are used to seeing. Keep in mind that while you confront change and undo some old habits, you don't have to abandon everything you once knew. Regard accepting change as a transitional phase that will ebb and flow like the tide, as long as you allow it to do so.

Develop a stress-management plan. We've devoted an entire chapter to the destructive effects of stress and how to prevent them. If your life is in transition, reread that chapter! It is universally understood that change is a thorny path. It always includes difficulties, many of which are hard or impossible to foresee. So take a proactive approach. Set aside some time to develop tactics for dealing with difficulty before it arrives.

Stress-management plans usually begin with a look at how you have typically coped with stress in the past, and the answers might alarm you. Harmful coping mechanisms include self-medicating with alcohol or drugs, smoking, oversleeping, or putting things off as long as possible. These are all disastrous stopgap measures that only compound the stress that will slam you later.

When you're devising a stress-management plan to confront change, you might also want to learn some relaxation techniques, get more physical activity, and shift toward a healthier diet. The better you feel overall, the less impact stress will have.

Identify the positives. Some of the most profound lessons of the class-act lifestyle are so straightforward. They seem almost too simple to be true. "Is the glass half-empty or half-full?" How you answer discloses more than just what you see. It reveals who you are.

Electric power would not be possible were it not for the resistance in the wires. A great shot in tennis can't be made without a net. No child learns to walk without falling down hundreds if not thousands of times. Virtually everything in our lives illustrates the interwoven nature of accomplishment and difficulty. So, ultimately, the glass is neither half-empty nor half-full. It's both at the same time. It has always been and will always be.

Start acting on necessary changes. Now you've come to terms with change by accepting it; you've configured some plans to manage the inevitable stress you'll endure; and you've identified some positive results that may come out of this change. In short, you have reduced a major change into a less intimidating set of smaller changes.

Now you're ready to start implementing those changes. You're not just waiting for change to befall you. Whether it's paperwork, things to throw away, decisions to make, or adaptations to absorb, dive into them. Don't take the passive route that says, "I'll deal with that when the time comes." Bear in mind that change is rarely assimilated in an instant. Time can be your ally, so let time do its work.

As the process takes place, you will make mistakes. We've

discussed the importance of forgiving yourself for bad tactical decisions. But other levels of mistakes can be more difficult to integrate as you work to become an unforgettable person. Some things you will deeply regret. Some actions will cause you to feel guilty, perhaps for many years. How should you deal with that?

A burdened conscience is painful, and life can be more difficult until you find a solution to your self-judgment. The good news is that the need to clear your conscience implies the *existence* of your conscience. You're not an uncaring sociopath. You're a decent person who's made some mistakes. You're a class act, or you're becoming one.

Clearing your conscience—forgiving yourself at an emotional or even a spiritual level—is often no easy task. But doing so is critical. Here are some steps you can take toward that worthwhile end.

Zero in on what's bothering you. The first step to clear your conscience is to isolate what's eating at you. Sometimes it's hard to admit to exactly what that is. As a result, it floats around the mind like a cloud of toxic fumes, growing more ominous each time we avoid it. Use honest language to define this cloud. See it in stark, unencumbered terms so you can isolate its precise nature.

In Shakespeare's *King Richard III*, the king takes until the last act to confront his conscience—or his conscience confronts him. He dreams that all the people he killed on his way to becoming king return, one at a time, and tell him he'll die in battle the next day. He wakes up and shouts, "O coward conscience, how dost thou afflict me!" By then, it's too late. Had he isolated his demons, he could have had a good night's sleep and been well rested when he faced the earl of Richmond on the battlefield. Instead, he not only lost his crown, but his life. But really, he'd already lost it. Don't let that happen to you!

Safely confess. As long as guilt is kept to yourself, it lives off your own life energy. You need to put a stop to that. Bring your feelings out into the open, but do so in a safe and controlled manner. That might mean a conversation with a close friend, a teacher, a parent, or a therapist. An interim step might be writing in a journal. However you choose to proceed, you should be determined to connect not only with the facts but with your feelings as well. In the safe environment you choose, "wear your heart on your sleeve." Make the experience as cathartic as you can. To the extent you're able to do this, the cloud that's hovered inside you will begin to dissipate.

But approach this experience carefully. Once more, Shakespeare was on top of this. In *Romeo and Juliet*, Juliet chose to unburden herself about her illicit love to her busybody nurse, who hustled off to tell Romeo like a sixteenth-century gossip. Tragic consequences were the result. In *Hamlet*, King Claudius purges his conscience about killing Hamlet's father through prayer, but he makes the mistake of praying out loud within earshot of Hamlet.

Put the universe back together! Erasing guilt can benefit by your balancing your negative action with an inversely positive one. Simply put, do the opposite of your previous ill. For example, if you kicked the neighbor's dog, volunteer at the pound. However, should performing the inverse prove impractical, find some form of atonement that will at once satisfy this step without placing additional burdens on your conscience and causing you (or someone else) more trouble. Psychologically, this is an important principle.

Wash your hands . . . literally. Ritual has an important place in emotional change, even if the ritual is informal and of your own creation.

Having atoned for your actions, clear your conscience and wash your hands. This is obviously a ceremonial step, but it has merit.

According to a study by researchers in Toronto and Chicago, "Physical cleansing alleviates the upsetting consequences of unethical behavior and reduces threats to one's moral self-image."

Literature's most famous—and frustrated—hand-washer is Lady Macbeth. While sleepwalking, she's plagued by her conscience and tries to wash the imaginary spots of King Duncan's blood off her hands. The cursed woman fails, and her sleepy chattering outs herself and her husband as murderers.

This should surprise no one: she neglected to confront her misdeeds in honest language, she purged herself in a public and vocal manner, she made no attempt to restore the universe, and when she *did* wash her hands in a ceremonial manner, she neglected actual soap and water.

But suppose none of this works—what then?

"I can't stop thinking about it." We all know this frustration, when it can mean a tough workday, a recently departed girlfriend, or a nerve-racking upcoming event. Whatever the case, we'll be better off the moment we bring peace to our thoughts.

This is frustrating because it's taking place inside you, within your physical and emotional self. Yet despite this intimate connection with your own anxiety, at times you feel unable to prevent it and helpless to correct it. Biologically, the underlying reason for this might be that certain regions of the brain are inaccessible to conscious intervention. That's an interesting concept, but it won't make you feel much better.

Some of the world's great spiritual traditions have found ways to address this. So have the insights of cognitive therapy and other psychological approaches. As difficult as it may be to attain peace of mind, the brain remains a neuroplastic organ. If it can change for the worse, it can also change for the better.

What can you do toward fostering that positive change?

Set aside time and space. The first step to quiet your mind is almost universal in the practice of meditation: establishing a time and a place to carry it out. *Meditation* is a loaded word. To the uninitiated, it may conjure up mystical practices of the Far East. But it has gained hard-earned credibility in the West as well. Meditation is widely regarded as effective in both psychological and physiological therapies. But it requires that you show the quieting of your mind some respect—and prove to yourself that you're serious about it—by setting aside a little bit of your time and energy so that your effort is sincere.

See the target clearly. We began this chapter with a discussion of goal setting, and we'll reach the end by setting the goal of a quiet mind. The full spectrum of mental activity isn't the target, just that poisoned frequency. Go ahead and relax any attempt to hold back even the most vivid and inflammatory thoughts and images related to what's making you uneasy.

Anchor your concentration. This is an intermediate step that promotes focused concentration on a chosen object. The principle is quite clear. The human mind can only process one thought at a time. If you're fully concentrating on a single object, you can't also be thinking about something else. Furthermore, the principle works with words as well as objects. If your mind is focused on a word, or even a meaningless syllable, it can't also be fretting and worrying. Can you see the powerful implications of this? By anchoring your thoughts on some neutral sight or sound, you can prevent them from drifting off in a direction that gives you discomfort.

One of the best techniques along these lines is to focus on your own breathing. Technically, it couldn't be easier. Just sit quietly and become "mindful" of inhaling and exhaling. In practice, you will be surprised by the number of distractions that crop up even if you're sitting by yourself in a completely quiet room. Your thoughts will begin to race. But that's the whole point. As you become aware of the ceaseless static that your brain is broadcasting to itself, you can begin to grasp the degree of psychic agitation this causes. But it's become such a constant presence in your life that you're not even aware of it.

Well, once you do become aware of it, you can see the benefits of quieting all this down. That's the purpose of meditation. It allows you to step outside yourself and perceive your incessant thoughts with the detachment of an outsider.

CHAPTER EIGHTEEN

Achievement, Productivity, and Beyond

Most personal development books begin with a focus on real-world achievement. That can take many forms, from goal setting, to wealth building, to ascending the corporate ladder. But we're saving achievement for last—not because it's unimportant, but because it's the culmination of everything a class act strives for. No class act would want material rewards without earning those rewards—and earning them is something class acts definitely know how to do. They deliver even more than they promise. They do it even sooner than was agreed upon. And if they don't make it look easy, they at least seem to enjoy the challenges. In short, class acts are real achievers emotionally, spiritually, and almost always financially. By the end of this chapter, you'll know more about how to gain those results, and you'll also have the tools to achieve them.

Some people in the world think they're entitled to make a lot of money. But many people still feel conflicted about it, though often unconsciously. Some of these people are financially successful. Some can make millions, others can make billions. But if making money for oneself is the only end, this generally leads to melancholy and disappointment regardless of the amounts involved. Being rich is not the same thing as having class, let alone having happiness.

To learn more about this rule, consult the biographies of extremely wealthy individuals such as John D. Rockefeller, William Randolph Hearst, or J. Paul Getty. For all their money, there is no way these could be described as happy men. A notable exception was Andrew Carnegie, who began life as an impoverished immigrant from Scotland and went on to lead the Carnegie Steel Company. Carnegie lived in the late nineteenth century, a time when the American economy was dominated by a small group of extremely wealthy individuals, of whom Carnegie was one of the wealthiest. But while John D. Rockefeller used to give away dimes, Andrew Carnegie used the majority of his fortune to build libraries and other cultural institutions all across America. To see the differences this made in these two men, just look at any photos taken of them toward the end of their lives. As we know, a picture is worth a thousand words!

Several years ago one of the major business schools did a study of some successful companies and corporations. One of the study's findings concerned the purpose for which these organizations came into being. At the start, the mission of each company was beyond just making a profit. It was about creating some larger benefit that extended beyond the boundaries of the company itself. Companies with that definition of success got to the top and stayed there. They didn't just do well for a while and then disappear. They remained in a higher place for the longest time. Sony, for example, was one of these companies, and Sony had several missions that were not expressed in financial terms. One was to elevate the perception of Japan as a society throughout the world, but most important it was to elevate the Japanese themselves. This purpose was certainly achieved, and other kinds of success came along with it.

Fundamentally, the laws of success are fair. Some people may have good or bad luck at the beginning of their career, but things even out over time. One of the most basic laws is productivity equals achievement. The more productive you are with your time, your skills, and your resources, the greater your achievement will be. Therefore, the question of how to actually be more productive is important.

If you're like most people, you can definitely improve your productivity, both at work and away from it. In the workplace, you can learn to streamline, consolidate, expedite, and better execute your responsibilities. Away from the workplace, you can learn to really relax and enjoy yourself, so that when you again called upon to produce, you can do so at full efficiency.

With these two facts in mind, we'll focus the first part of this chapter on techniques for improving you career productivity—especially your use of the most important career resource of all, which is your *time.* Then we'll conclude with a look at how to optimize your life away from the workplace. To be a class act, you definitely need to have both these elements working together.

WHAT IS YOUR DAY LIKE?

Right now, think about your job. What do you do first thing in the morning? How many breaks do you take? Do you have idle time, or do you barely have enough time to finish your assignments? Both of these options are bad news. The first one places you in a lethargic holding pattern. The second is a ticket to emotional and physical burnout, probably sooner rather than later. So in the spirit of good career health and work-life balance, let's explore some class-act ideas for enhanced productivity.

First, learn not just to organize, but to prioritize. Despite how it may seem in the moment, life is full of seeming urgencies that don't really matter in the long run. Technology has increased our sense of urgency. A FedEx letter cries for more immediate attention than something sent bulk rate, and a fax outshouts even a FedEx. But the delivery system has no bearing on the importance of the content. Maybe you're four minutes late for a staff meeting, but the meeting itself could be a waste of everybody's time.

Unless you take conscious control of the process, you'll tend to react to apparent urgency, even if it's relatively unimportant. What's even worse, you may miss what's important unless it also carries a sense of urgency.

To avoid this, develop a way to *interrupt* yourself several times a day. Just stop what you're doing and ask yourself, "Is this how I want or need to spend my time right now?" If the answer is yes, go back to what you were doing. You will have affirmed your decision consciously.

Here's another possibility. You're doing something you want or need to do, but not at this moment. So put it aside in favor of something that's more time sensitive. That way you'll avoid getting caught in deadline pressure later.

And if you neither want nor need to be doing it, now or ever—just stop! It may surprise you, but if you stick with the "want/need" question for a few days, you will catch yourself doing things you can't justify doing, and you'll find yourself making changes to better serve your needs.

Next, learn to recognize when time *isn't* the problem. Even if going to that staff meeting is neither important nor pleasurable, it may be a lot easier than confronting the deadlines that are hanging over your head. And confronting the deadlines may be easier than trying to solve the problems in your relationships. Often we take the path of least resistance, especially if we can justify the choice—as in, "I had to go to the meeting. The deadline will have to get pushed back."

Whatever you do, stop looking for *more* time. You'll never find more time. It isn't lost, and there isn't any more of it. You're living in it. You have to consciously decide to live it in certain ways and not others. You have to use time wisely by taking it away from one activity and giving it to another.

As we discussed earlier, conscientious and creative use of a to-do list can help here. If you want to exercise three times a week, if you need to do some long-range career and financial planning, if you care enough about another human being to want to strengthen your relationship, then schedule time for these things. Otherwise, you may not get to them—or you'll only get to them when your energy and focus are low.

Another powerful suggestion for determining your priorities is deceptively simple. Buy a little notebook that you can carry around in your pocket. You can buy an expensive leather Day-Timer if you want, but a cheap spiral notebook will do just as well. Over five working days, use the notebook to determine your priorities. It will take some diligence, but make the effort—because this is probably the single most important thing you can do toward really setting priorities in your life.

Paying attention to how you spend your day will automatically cause you to make changes. It's a fundamental principle of modern physics that observation changes reality. It may even be that observation *creates* reality—but for now let's just say that keeping this diary will cause you to alter your behavior in some positive ways, guaranteed. That's just from keeping a conventional time diary, in which you track the amount of time you spend on various tasks—or maybe in avoiding various tasks. But now we're going to introduce some refinements that will hugely multiply the power of this tool.

In addition to tracking your phone calls and lunch dates, use your diary to track your reactive and proactive behaviors over a week. A simple way to do this is just to write a *P* or an *R* beside the different entries. For example, if you get put on hold by a client for fifteen minutes and then you're so annoyed that you almost lose the order, put an *R* in the margin. And if you see a chance to share with another person and you take advantage of that opportunity, write a *P.*

It's that simple—but what do you think will happen? I promise you that over the week the *P*'s will start to multiply and the *R*'s will start to diminish. And it will seem effortless. That's how powerful the time diary can be.

After you've kept the diary for a week, read through it with real attention. What does it tell you? What do you learn about your priorities—not in terms of what you think they are, but in how you actually use your time? If you're a parent, for instance, you may feel that it's important to spend positive time with your children. Most parents do feel that way, but many find that they act upon those feelings a lot less than they intended to. You may desire to do some volunteer work to help people less fortunate than yourself, but does your time diary show that you've acted upon that intention? The chances are, a lot more of your time has been devoted to one detail after another. But don't worry, because you're going to keep the diary for a second week. And in the second week you're going to be much more proactive about how you use your time.

SPACE AND TIME

Einstein showed that the concepts of space and time are actually inseparable. Just as you organize your priorities, organize the physical space in which you spend your time. Clutter can have a major negative impact on your productivity. Despite the obvious benefits of a clean work area, few people take the time to file and organize—so I suggest you get on it. Take an hour at the end of the day to find a place for important items. File them away in a space that is easy to access and remember. If more than thirty days has gone by since your last use of a paper or a file, purge it from your space. It may be painful but it's well worth the effort.

Learn to save personal affairs for your own time. You may not realize the ripple effect that an occasional personal call can have on your day. The impact can be very detrimental. So be vigilant about personal interruptions and your work will get done a lot faster.

Be thought-intensive in the morning and labor-intensive in the afternoon. Most people are mentally sharper before lunch, so try to be done with mentally challenging tasks as early as possible. If you have to crunch numbers or write an extensive report, get started on it as soon as you reach your desk. Schedule meetings and conference calls in the afternoon. This is the best time to interact and share ideas.

Become an expert delegator. You may not have a team of people to manage, but it's still vital to make best use of your colleagues' help. Take a look at your tasks and find out where your coworkers can be of use.

It's so easy to tell people about their weak points. Weak points are almost always obvious, at least to other people—in fact, that's why they're weak! Our weaknesses are the things we can't hide, except sometimes from ourselves. But what happens if you keep dwelling on weaknesses when you're dealing with a particular individual? What is the effect of constantly calling attention to areas that need improvement? Even if the criticism is completely accurate, the result will be insecurity and fear. Positive change will not take place at a fundamental level. At best, there will be some improvement so as to avoid further criticism. But that's not the same thing as real change. To bring about real change, a leader needs to connect with an individual's inner aspirations, and to locate the points where those are congruent with the goals of the entire organization.

To put it more simply, you've got to find out what people want, and what they're good at, then invite them to put those skills to work both for themselves and for the group as a whole.

THE DIFFERENCE BETWEEN RIGHT AND WRONG

Fixing what's wrong, therefore, is most often a matter of discovering what's right. It's not correcting weaknesses, it's building on strengths. Make this your goal with other people and with yourself as well. Judging yourself almost always leads to negativity: "I'm incompetent, I'm unintelligent, I'm just plain bad!" We rarely think of the things we're good at or that we enjoy. If you enjoy playing baseball, it won't bother you that you're not as good as a major leaguer—because the experience is its own reward. But suppose you have to stop playing baseball for eight hours every day and do bookkeeping or electrical wiring or piano tuning. Suppose you have to give up what you love to do something that makes money, and that might not even be anything you're particularly good at. What will be the result? You'll judge yourself on your obligations, and you may also see your real talents as just a recreation or even a self-indulgence.

But suppose you were able to devote all your time to what you enjoy. Instead of your seeing that activity as a mere pastime, suppose someone could show you how to connect it to your career—to the objectives of your company or organization? If that happened, you would most likely improve at your real skill much faster than at something that was just done to pay the bills. What's more, you would feel better about yourself and about the employer who gave you this wonderful opportunity.

Giving people just that kind of opportunity is an essential quality of an effective manager and an unforgettable person. Finding a way to *make* that opportunity is a key attribute of employees who intend to genuinely give and share what's best in themselves. When these qualities and attributes are put into action, the result is productivity and achievement for everyone.

We've spoken at some length about how to achieve more through workplace productivity. But work is not an end in itself. One purpose of work is to be able to enjoy your life *away* from work. If you follow the suggestions you're read so far, you'll definitely have more of that time away. Now let's see how you can make that time more fulfilling.

Here's a useful exercise you can do every day to connect the events of your life to the bigger picture. Most people tend to see financial matters and career issues as if they were in a world of their own. If we have a disagreement with a supervisor at work, we don't make a connection between that and anything else. We don't connect it to a similar disagreement with a spouse or a close friend. If we forget to pay the electric bill, we don't relate that to something else we may have been worried about. Most important, we don't see how seemingly minor events can actually be sign-posts with significant information.

This exercise is designed to remedy those oversights, and it's simple. At the end of every business day, ask yourself a single question: "What have I learned?"

Write this question down, then answer it in writing also. The best time to do this is whenever you're ready to end your work-day, because you want this to be focused specifically on what you learned while you were working—while you were doing whatever you do to earn a living. People tend to set aside this area from the other parts of their life—from the more obviously emotional relationships with family and friends, for example. But this is also the foundation for becoming a class act. So make an effort to see your workday as more than just a matter of dollars and cents. What did you learn in your work during the past eight or ten hours? What were the messages, and how can you relate them to the bigger picture of your life?

Your answer can take many forms. It can be a practical lesson, or it can be something much more spiritual. It's unfortunate when people go through their lives with a hazy sense of their dreams and goals, but they ignore the connection between those goals and what happens every day. So writing down what you've learned is a good way of making those connections, and it's an important step toward being an unforgettable person. This exercise will definitely move you in that direction.

By reaching the end of this book, you've not only shown a sincere interest in becoming a class act, you've also proven that in many respects you already are one. On behalf of the entire Dale Carnegie organization, I hope that these chapters will prove useful to you, and even unforgettable. May they help you to become the prosperous and totally fulfilled person that you deserve to be.

Epilogue

A single, unifying theme runs though all of Dale Carnegie's work: Life is what you make of it. Whatever may lie in your past or your future, you are in control of how you respond right now. Everything comes down to the choice you make each day and each moment.

To help you make the best choices for yourself and for everyone around you, here in closing are some quotes from Dale Carnegie.

If you have a worry problem, do three things: First, ask yourself, "What is the worst that can possibly happen?" Second, prepare to accept that outcome if you have to. Third, calmly proceed to improve on the worst.

Why does such a simple thing as keeping busy help to drive out anxiety? It's because of psychology's most fundamental laws: that is, it is utterly impossible for any human mind, no matter how brilliant, to think of more than one thing at any given time.

Fatigue is most often caused not by work, but by worry, frustration, and resentment.

All the king's horses and all the king's men can't put the past back together again. So let's remember: don't try to saw sawdust.

Don't fuss about trifles. Don't permit little things to ruin your happiness.

Put a "stop-loss" order on your worries. Decide just how much anxiety a thing may be worth and refuse to give it any more.

Use the law of averages to outlaw your worries. Ask yourself, "What are the odds against this thing's happening at all?"

Get the facts. Let's not even attempt to solve our problems without first collecting all the facts in an impartial manner.

A well-known legal maxim says de minimis non curat lex, *"the law does not concern itself with trifles," and neither should we if we want peace of mind.*

When we have accepted the worst, we have nothing more to lose. And that automatically means we have everything to gain!

Do you remember the things you were worrying about a year ago? How did they work out? Didn't you waste a lot of fruitless energy on account of most of them? Didn't most of them turn out right after all?

If you were to read everything that has ever been written about worry by the great philosophers of the universe, you would never read anything more profound than "Don't cross your bridges until you come to them" and "Don't cry over spilt milk."

If you have worries, there is no better way to eliminate them than by walking them off. Just take them out for a walk. They may take wings and fly away!

If you can't sleep, then get up and do something instead of lying there and worrying. It's the worry that gets you, not the sleep.

Give your problem all the thought you possibly can before a solution is reached. But when the matter is settled and over, worry not at all.

If we can't have all we want, let's not poison our days with worry and resentment. Let's be good to ourselves. Let's be philosophical. And philosophy, according to Epictetus, boils down to this: "The essence of philosophy is that a man should so live that his happiness shall depend as little as possible on external things."

Put a BIG, broad, honest-to-God smile on your face; throw back your shoulders; take a good, deep breath; and sing a snatch of a song. If you can't sing, whistle. If you can't whistle, hum. You will quickly discover that it is physically impossible to remain blue or depressed while you are acting out the symptoms of being radiantly happy!

When we hate our enemies, we are giving them power over us: power over our sleep, our appetites, our blood pressure, our health, and our happiness. Our enemies would dance with joy if only they knew how they were worrying us, lacerating us, and getting even with us! Our hatred is not hurting them at all, but our hate is turning our own days and nights into a hellish turmoil.

If you and I don't keep busy—if we sit around and brood—we will hatch out a whole flock of what Charles Darwin used to call the wibber-gibbers. And the wibber-gibbers are just old-fashioned gremlins that will run us hollow and destroy our power of action and our power of will.

About 90 percent of the things in our lives are right and about 10 percent are wrong. If we want to be happy, all we have to do is to concentrate on the 90 percent that are right and ignore the 10 percent that are wrong. If we want to be worried and bitter and have stomach ulcers, all we have to do is to concentrate on the 10 percent that are wrong and ignore the 90 percent that are glorious.

About the Author

Dale Carnegie was born in 1888 in Missouri. He wrote his now-renowned book, *How to Win Friends and Influence People,* in 1936—a milestone that cemented the rapid spread of his core values across the United States. During the 1950s, the foundations of Dale Carnegie Training as it exists today began to take form. Dale Carnegie himself passed away soon after in 1955, leaving his legacy and set of core principles to be disseminated for decades to come.

Today, Dale Carnegie Training partners with middle-market and large corporations, as well as organizations, to produce measurable business results by improving the performance of employees with emphasis on leadership, sales, team-member engagement, customer service, presentations, process improvement, and other essential management skills. Recently identified by the *Wall Street Journal* as one of the top twenty-five high-performing franchises, the Dale Carnegie Training programs are available in more than twenty-five languages throughout the entire United States and in more than eighty countries. Dale Carnegie Training includes as its clients four hundred of the Fortune 500 companies. Approximately 7 million people have experienced Dale Carnegie Training. For more information, please visit www.dalecarnegie.com.